CRAFT HIS FALL AND TAKE IT ALL

Karen LeBarron

From Us. For Us.

Contents

LEGAL DISCLAIMER

Neither the publisher nor the author is engaged in rendering professional advice or services to the reader. This book contains observations of situations within divorce and custody proceedings. The contents provided within this book are not intended as a substitute for seeking professional help. This book is not a legal dictionary. There are countless attorneys, books and other resources that do an outstanding job explaining the numerous important intricacies of a person's state or country's divorce and custody laws. It is advised that each person hire their own competent divorce/custody attorney to help a person understand and navigate the laws of their state or country applicable to their specific situation(s). The contents of this book are not a substitute for hiring a competent divorce/custody lawyer.

The information presented within this book are for informational purposes only. This book does not support, nor condone, any criminal plans or activities. It is the hope that these observations will help reveal many of the different chains of events and intracacies, thereby reducing paralyzing fears victims may be experiencing to help them initiate the freedom they deserve. A predator is a master at closing and isolating a victim from the world. Neither the publisher nor the author shall be held liable or responsible for any loss or damage allegedly arising from any information contained in this book. Regardless of appeared claims made within this book – the author does not make any claims. Seek legal advice. **You**, and **you** alone, are responsible for each decision **you** make. Do not jeopardize the sharing of this growing collection of experiences that will help countless others. From us. For us.

INTRODUCTION

On the 10th of January in 49 BC Julius Caesar crossed the Rubicon with his legions. That was over two thousand years ago, and a man at that, so why should someone care? Because there is something powerful in looking at historic examples for inspiration. Even though Caesar had everything, he still faced seemingly insurmountable situations preventing him from taking more.

The Roman Senate had ordered Julius Caesar to release his armies and return home. His masters were beginning to question his motives and intentions. They publicly ordered him to not cross the northern river of the Rubicon with his army or face trial for treason. Little did they know Rome already belonged to him, and his soldiers were there for him to use to fulfil his desires. He ordered his pawns to cross that cold muddy river, and upon setting foot on that other shore, he stated, "the die is cast." As he broke out of his master's chains, he took it all. Destroying entire nations, men, women, and children.

As shown through Caesar's decision and countless others through the ages, wanting more is simply human nature. The mothers in this book also wanted more, and decided they deserved more. She thought to herself, what stands between me taking more? Do not the ends justify the means? She would no longer be tied down. Everything around her, everyone around her, would be better off if she did this. She would have to use everyone around her, but they would ultimately benefit from this as well in the end. She would no longer live in subjection underneath man, he who believes he is superior. She would arise and take what belongs to her.

How have mothers gone about taking everything that is

rightfully theirs? They removed their husbands from their lives, without murdering them of course. Oh, many have, but that is too risky and messy. They used their wits. They planned and executed. They crafted his fall and took it all. It was their Rubicon, their point of no return. Nothing was guaranteed. Success was always a gamble. Some risk was here and there, but there is a golden age within the American justice system that is balanced in favor of the mother. The courts even provided guidance along the way. No longer was this the age of man. Heterosexual men, believing themselves superior, no longer standing upon us with their toxicity. This is her time. Her time to arise and take what was hers. With the heart of a warrior princess, she visualized herself as a serpent, coiling into position around his neck, strangling the life out of her soon to be ex-husband. Figuratively, of course.

Many mothers choose to begin by making reports of physical abuse. This book is a compilation of observations attempting to be compiled into one flowing story. Far too many mothers act out during moments of great emotion and make permanently unfortunate decisions. But what good is it if the mother spends her life penniless, barely scraping by, or worse yet spending her life incarcerated? We are far too intelligent for that. The mother deserves to be able to enjoy watching the father suffer for the rest of his natural life. So she worked at having him incarcerated. She used the system that defines the mother as the weaker vessel. A system that does their best to cover up any wrongdoing the mother may commit to reach their end goal.

The children will be better off with her having sole custody. She does not intend to share custody with the father for the next 15 plus years. She did a risk assessment. It is widely estimated that more than 80% of allegations of abuse in divorce cases are indeed false allegations. The benefits are high when those allegations succeed, and when they are not completely successful repercussions are seemingly nonexistent. In her research she notices how even when the father does not end up in prison, there is still sweet success in how the father will be mentally, emotionally, financially, and physically destroyed. She also takes note of how due to the nature of the accusations, many of the fathers do not survive under the stress of these allegations, whether naturally or not.

She realizes elected judges will not take a chance the mother's allegations are anything less than truthful. She even tried to imagine a situation where a judge dismisses an allegation of child abuse, and then the worst happened. That judge's career would be thoroughly and absolutely finished. Consequently, when most allegations are proven false, they are quietly swept under the carpet so that no mother could be further afraid to seek help. The journey will be messy. Sacrifices will be required. But the ends justify the means.

So the mother took a trip with a friend and her children leaving a daughter behind, or a youngest son, home alone with the father. She tells the father that she is taking the other child(ren) with her and leaving the daughter with him so that she will not have to miss school, or some sort of appointment she has scheduled. The trip is scheduled to last two or more nights away. During this trip she emotionally leaned on her friend's shoulder discussing all the many horrible things in her life due to the father. She claims to be abused and scared for her safety, as well as that of her children. Within a couple nights of these intimate conversations, she has her friend so emotionally worked up that the two of them decide to rush back home to check on the child left behind.

What did she do when she got home? The mother cast her die. She forever crossed her Rubicon. She began crafting his fall so that she would get it all.

CHAPTER 1 – THE CAST

This chapter introduces the reader to many of the typical entities a mother will encounter through her journey. Her priority with these entities is to remain charismatic and build a web of support. The most beneficial members to flock to her support system are lonely single women between the ages of fifty to seventy that believe they are quite religious. Her group of friends will carry this torch with her until the end of time. They are invaluable. They will literally convince themselves that they are serving Christ Himself by giving her their time, their favor, and their money. Believing in their crusade, they will energetically engage everyone involved to motivate or to inform them of when they think they are missing the mark. The squeaky wheel gets the grease.

Emergency Room*

Medical — Pediatrician*

Urgent Care Clinics*

CPS*

GAL*

Law Enforcement* — Court Appointed Conflict Counselor

Investigation — Counsellors* — Court Appointed Child Counselor

The Mother — CAC

Private Investigators

Shelter* — Principal

School* — Counselor

Support — Nurse

Telephone Support Hotlines* — Teacher

Your Attorney* — Father's Attorney / The Father

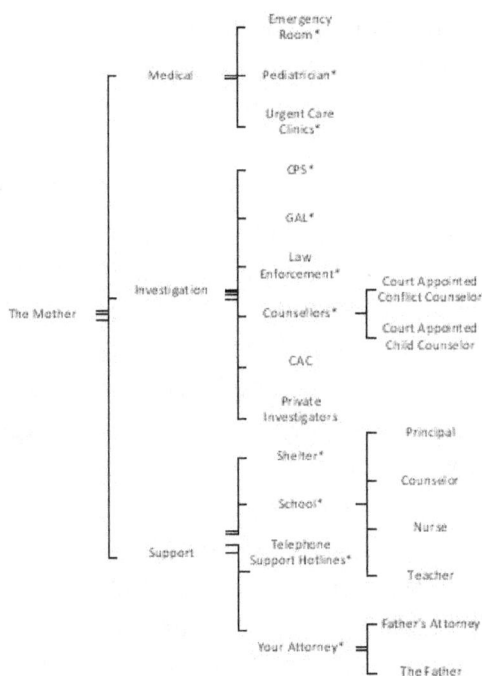

Figure 1 The cast, and who are the *Mandatory Reporters. the mother staggered on average one new allegation to a different entity approximately one per month.

There is supposedly separation of church and state, not when a mother has made allegations of sexual abuse against the father of his children. Even if the authorities become aware of her agenda, if she has a support group of church women behind her, she will receive the benefit of being delusional. There is strength in numbers. The beauty of being considered delusional is the judge will continuously claim, as fact, that the child made an accusation to the mother at least in the very beginning. Due to the traumatic nature of such a claim it had to have placed the caring mother into a state of panic, trauma, and further delusion. This provides the judge the ability to excuse all the mother's multiple and continuous allegations as well as prevent the authorities from holding the mother accountable. The mother will nearly always come before the children in the eyes of the current justice system.

The judge will not permit anyone in the trial to testify that the mother is delusional. It will be kept a convenient excuse off the record. If any subject matter expert witness, whether court appointed or not, attempts to state that the mother is delusional the judge will sternly state that is their personal opinion in an attempt to discredit decades of professional experiences for the record. She will dismiss and disrespect any expert witness' findings if they do not follow the desired narrative.

As far in advance of an allegation as the mother could manage, she had long been sowing seeds with as many people possible constructing her narrative that she was the glue that held the family together within a tumultuous home. She claimed that during that time of holding the family together she claimed her husband was physically or sexually abusing her and/or the children, but she was in denial, and did not think anyone would ever believe or help her. She says she faced years of name calling, humiliation, financial control, isolation, threats, etc. She began isolating the father as early as she could. The mother always remembered that even if law enforcement does become aware of her agenda, their hands are tied from pursuing any charges.

When the mother held conversations with these entities, she always had a game plan she followed. She tried to predict many different aspects. She created as many details as possible to construct believable memories. Her priority is making her husband have a negative outburst anywhere and anytime within the timeline of reaching divorce and custody, as well as beyond that. She is creating the largest stress on the father he has ever experienced. He cannot fight back. He is helpless. His suffering is paramount to her success. If her schemes can lead the father into exhibiting a negative outburst the judge will use that to justify every one of the mother's allegations. The judge will spin it in such a manner as he has shown himself to be unsafe and to have bad judgement. What do these negative outbursts look like? A negative outburst could be vocal or physical, it just needs to be observed and preferably recorded if possible. The mother tried to create opportunities to coax him into screaming at her, placing a finger on her, even stumbling and falling into his arms during a children exchange. She jumped into his car's driver's seat so that he was unable to leave hoping he would touch her arm. She even violently jerked the children from his arms. How wonderful she thinks if her children see him place a single finger on her. Anything to help her claim assault.

Many men that have been loyal for so many years to then be blind sided with these allegations will run into the arms of another woman, or women, before the divorce is over. Now the mother can accuse him of having other women in the marital home, or in the home with her children. The mother will sometimes make this claim even when not true. But men will be men, so it will most likely be something the mother can rightfully claim. This is just another item the judge can use to say the father has bad judgement, further supporting other allegations.

The mother will expect the destitute father to begin heavily drinking their situation away with alcohol, or even with illegal substances. Now the mother has a basis to make the accusation of him having addiction problems. How does an addict not continue their habit during custodial time? If the father does fall into this unfortunate rut, then the judge has another critical reason to label him having bad judgement, further supporting the mother's other allegations.

Below are some key descriptions the mother sometimes uses to describe the father to the entities involved. Please note this list is not at all comprehensive.

- He belittles and demeans me.
- He is only focused on himself and does not think about me nor my children.
- He carries unrealistic expectations. The mother can take this opportunity to accuse him of harboring sick fetishes that he tries to make her participate in.
- He has no empathy and dehumanizes others.
- He is hypocritical.
- He is manipulative and narcissistic.

- He directs my every move through financial threats.
- He gaslights me. The mother can dramatize how she sees the true him now, and how he had confused her through denials and promises that made her doubt reality. He nearly made me do something bad to myself because he had made me believing I was the one losing my mind.
- He is an obsessive liar.
- He has broken the trust and I just do not see how I can keep trying to rebuild the relationship all by myself.
- He is obsessed with his appearance and mine as well. The mother can say something like he either makes her dress to show her off like a piece of property, or he makes her dress like a vagabond so that no one will take notice of her.
- He is incapable of receiving criticism, but constantly puts me and/or my children down.
- His pride is easily wounded.
- He is envious of others.
- He has severe mood swings. The mother can say how she feels like he is truly bipolar because one moment he is vicious and then the next moment he is sweet as honey.
- He gives me the silent treatment, walking away when I tried to have constructive conversations.
- He blames me for everything. He never accepts responsibility and tells me everything is my fault.
- He threatens the safety of me and/or my children. The mother can claim he has guns and has even pointed one at me and/or my children. If the mother knows he does not have a gun, she can say she has reason to believe he has a friend that has given him one. Furthermore, she claims he has at times even placed a kitchen knife against her throat, possibly even claim that he placed a knife against her third trimester abdomen in the past.
- He expects my instantaneous and unfailing loyalty, but

never reciprocates it.

- He sabotages my educational or career aspirations. The mother can say he shows up at her place of work or drives by to keep her in line. She can say he calls, texts, or emails constantly through the day demanding immediate response.
- He has isolated me. He hates my friends. He is jealous. He gives me ultimatums to remove myself from friends or coworkers or face the threat of some sort of consequence(s).
- I have always had to walk around on eggshells throughout my marriage or face being slapped, taken sexually against my will, etc.

The mother began building her story as far in advance of the divorce as possible. The mother shared her alleged fears with everyone within her network, as well as people she knew within his workplace. She built the story with her doctor, and her children's pediatrician.

The mother had always heard that all is fair in love and war. As the mother accused him of the worst things a father could ever do to a child, he was incapacitated. Whether he is an alpha male or not, he will be brought into a submissive beta male position throughout this process, or he will negatively react. If and when he does have a negative reaction the judge will pin the mother's allegations right on his chest. The mother crafted his fall and took it all.

The mother will have control of the finances. Due to the nature of sexual allegations people will trip over themselves to not only assist the mother, but they will make things easier for her and often take responsibilities upon themselves. Older men will do all her chores, fixing her car, etc. seeing her as their sweet little girl. Older women will share all their experiences of what does and does not work. Some will even help the mother coach and alienate her children from their father. The mother took advantage of multiple churches. Not just one. Spreading the word.

Her inner circle, her closest advisers, primarily consisted of church people, and for lack of better word sugar daddies and sugar mamas. She will interact with medical entities, counsellors, the Child Advocacy Center, Child Protective Services, and Law Enforcement. She met the staff and women at the shelter she stayed in for battered women and children before her husband was kicked out of his home. She kept her children's teachers aware of the trauma the children are going through due to their father. Both the mother and father had attorneys. And she used the father's finances to fund a private investigator to gather information on him for her use. And the case was overseen by a judge.

Many of the entities are mandatory reporters. Mandatory reporters are required to report the mother's accusations of sexual abuse to the authorities. The mothers had a successful strategy of staggering a new allegation to a different mandatory reporter approximately once a month, and sometimes multiple allegations within one reporting over the years of the process. She rotated the entities so that she did not exhaust one entity too often.

Medical

Due to the nature of the allegations, the mother will have many interactions with medical professionals. The mother began carrying out her agenda well in advance. While the father served her, she scheduled doctor visits with her general practitioner, her OBGYN, and made accusations of different types of abuse for documentation but not too far as to be reported so that she could keep the marriage together. The mother began softly suggesting emotional abuse, control, manipulation, stress, anxiety, to herself and what seemed to be also directed toward the children at times by the father. The mother stated these things as being in the past, with no witness, keeping them as things that a mandatory reporter, such as these doctors, would not be required to report. The mother made sure that the doctors and the insurance blocked the husband from having access to insurance claims made on her behalf. She constructed a medical history of long occurring alleged abuses. Meanwhile the father had no clue.

The mother made her initial reportable allegation by taking her child(ren) to the emergency room to report that she left her child with the father while she went away for a few nights and upon her return she noticed a difference in her child's behavior. At this time she referenced the history of abuses she had previously shared with doctors. The emergency room doctors, with the assistance of nurses and technicians, will look for abuse indicators that they are trained and experienced to look for. These indicators provide them with additional information on what to look for next, or not. The mother did not have to try to influence any indicators. Her reporting of a change in behavior, claims of past abuses, and then the Protection from Abuse Order she immediately filed places the burden of proof on the father. The court will always weigh on the side of caution. They cannot permit a child to stay with a potential predator, so he is kicked out of their lives, until an investigation lasting months, or years, is completed.

The child will likely have medical examinations performed by the Child Advocacy Center and checked on by school nurses while they are in school. The child's teacher and school administration will have the school nurse looking for any signs of abuse throughout the day at every chance they can get because often children will make statements at unpredictable times and situations, especially in environments they are comfortable in.

Immediately after the mother filed the PFA she also filed for divorce. The power lies with the one to file divorce. This places the father permanently as the defendant through the case. Therefore, during the divorce, especially if the father has regained any form of unsupervised custody, the mother can visit the child's pediatrician and report further strange observations about her child so that the child will be analyzed more. All this chaos creates more confusion in the child, which created changes in behavior some of the mother's influenced counsellors have been looking for. The child will forget things, and this loss of memory will allow the judge to claim that the child's brain is trying to suppress traumatic events. The mother does not worry about the child because she has always been told a child is resilient. As far as the mother is concerned, the more they are questioned about sexual matters, and the more they are looked at privately, they will eventually become more malleable to her agenda.

The mother visited multiple doctors. She will visit urgent care clinics and those referred to as docs in the box. She will look until she finds at least one that she can overwhelm with concern and cause to note in the child's medical record of observing at least one indicator of abuse. This will cause the doctor to report an additional accusation to Child Protective Services, beginning a new investigation. It is not critical for anyone to observe any indicators though.

Investigation

Child Protective Services (CPS.)

Child Protective Services, or CPS, is a branch of the mother's state's social services department. They are responsible for the assessment, investigation, and intervention of alleged child abuse and neglect, including sexual abuse. They, along with doctors, is where the mother reported her allegations of abuse and neglect. They investigate and help prevent child abuse. They help in protecting children from physical and emotional harm. They ensure children are receiving proper supervision and medical care.

- What the mother will need to be prepared to report for the CPS report:
  - identify the child, or children, allegedly being abused
  - the child's address
  - mother's telephone number
  - identity of each person living in the same home with the abused child(ren)
  - identify the predator
  - identify the allegation he has done and to

whom
- describe the abuse or neglect
- describe how it affected the child(ren) such as injury and/or change in behavior
- dates of the alleged abuse
- report how she learned of the abuse
- is it physical abuse, neglect, sexual abuse, abandonment, emotional abuse, or a combination thereof?
- Are there any witnesses?
- Which hospital(s) and doctor(s) treated the injuries?
- List all prior abuses.
- What school does her child(ren) attend?
- Is it safe for the Child Protective Services to visit the home? Possibly this answer is no because he has weapons, or he has threatened her with kitchen knives, etc.
- Possible indicators
    - Burns
    - Bites
    - Bruises
    - black eyes
    - fear
    - anxiety
    - depression
    - withdrawn
    - aggressiveness
    - doesn't want to go home
    - withdrawn from adults
    - appetite changes
    - differences in sleeping schedule
    - child being mean to pets
    - nightmares
    - bedwetting
    - sophisticated knowledge of something

sexual
- running away from home
- interest in strangers
- difficulty walking or sitting
- marks in private area
- sudden dislike for school

The mother did not unrealistically expect herself to be prepared to answer every question, but she did answer as many as possible. In the beginning of her journey, she did stumble and forget things at times. But people do whatever it takes to help a mother in distress over claims her children are being sexually abused. She learned new things and clever ways to report future allegations as she visited each entity.

CPS's Child Abuse/Neglect Report (CA/N) is the report that contains the mother's submitted report that she made in person, or over the phone. It is built on the narrative, court reports, photographs, and correspondence. Once the initial assessment is completed the child welfare personnel will record the abuse indicated, or not indicated. CA/N reports are distributed to the appropriate investigative agencies, with discussions ongoing with the District Attorney's office, in accordance with standard operating procedures with the local law enforcement agencies. CPS and Law Enforcement will share any necessary photographs to document injuries, or lack thereof. Child protective services has a timeline required for each type of allegation of child abuse. CPS and Law Enforcement are on-call at all hours for emergency situations. Timing is to the mother's advantage, because often inexperienced rookies are the ones having to take the night and weekend shifts.

When CPS receives a report, they will investigate to determine if a child has been abused or neglected. CPS will determine what steps need to be carried out to protect the child(ren) from immediate danger. CPS will assess the risk of any continuing danger to the children. CPS will decide what interventions are needed to keep the child safe, and implement these steps, sometimes with the help of other agencies or programs. They will also decide any need for ongoing support of the family such as case management, counseling, and medical care.

The mother was prepared to answer the CPS front end worker regarding the following to build the case.
- Does the child have trouble walking or sitting?
- Is the child suddenly refusing to participate in physical activities?
- Is the child having nightmares?
- Is the child wetting the bed?
- Is there a change in appetite?
- Is the child demonstrating bizarre sexual knowledge or behavior?
- Has the child run away from home when she is not home?
- Is the child attaching very quickly to strangers or new adults in their environment?

Obviously, the mother will claim that her child has reported sexual abuse by the father to herself. The burden of proof will permanently lie on the shoulders of the father. The justice system will ensure there is no way that this can be disproven. The mother will never have to prove her child made such a claim.

The mother will also need to be prepared to answer some things she is noticing about the child's father.
- Is he unduly protective of the child or is he severely limiting the child's contact with other children, especially of the opposite sex?
- Has he become secretive and isolated?
- Is he jealous, or controlling, with family members? Manipulative? Narcissistic? Etc.

Childwelfare.gov is a great tool for learning how, when, where to report child abuse and where to seek support groups.

CPS will assess the mother's report and determine

whether it meets statutory and agency guidelines for which type of investigation. The investigation will result in a finding of Substantiated/Indicated, or it will be Ruled Out/Unsubstantiated/Not Indicated. To the judge it will not matter if abuse is determined to be not indicated. The mother will have the benefit of the doubt, and to many the father will forever be branded a pedophile.

Guardian ad Litem

Within such high conflict custody cases a judge will usually assign a Guardian ad Litem, GAL, to the case. It is said the GAL is the children's attorney. The GAL is supposed to protect the rights and interests of the children above any narratives being pressed from the mother, the father, and even that of a judge. The GAL is supposed to neutrally investigate the facts of the case. They have the authority to review the children's school, medical, and mental health records. The GAL will interview people involved from witnesses, teachers, doctors, counsellors, CPS, and discuss matters with the mother and father's attorneys. Following the investigation, the GAL will typically testify at the divorce and custody trial making recommendations to the judge on matters concerning the children.

While the mother can assume the judge will appoint a GAL, if the father's attorneys have the wherewithal to request and nominate a fair GAL they may very well do so. This would not be in the mother's best interest. If the father's attorneys nominate a fair GAL, the judge may not feel they are able to reject him or her due to the lack of a basis to do so. However, the mother can nip this possibility in the bud and have her attorneys request a GAL early in the case. The mother should have her attorneys nominate a GAL that they have a working and personal relationship so that they are able to get as much influential time with the GAL as possible. This will provide the judge the opportunity to nominate the GAL that is influenced by the mother's attorneys, and possibly the judge, to control the intended narrative. A GAL in the mother's favor can also provide her protection from CPS and other investigators. Furthermore, the father will typically be ordered to pay the GAL's fees, at least until the divorce is finalized.

Most investigators have very brief interactions with the mother. They follow up on the allegations and then will seemingly vanish. The GAL does not go away. Since the GAL is involved throughout this long process the GAL may take some occasional positions opposing the mother. The mother will be advised to not antagonize the GAL, but this is unnecessary advice. The GAL's bottom line is typically met by the judge assigning cases to that GAL. The court system's objective is for the mother to have sole custody. This position enables the mother's decisions and makes efforts to ensure the narrative remains on track. A GAL can go so far as to direct social workers, mandatory reporters, to not report some of the mother's dozens of allegations to ensure that the possibility of delusion is not replaced with maliciousness in the eyes of law enforcement. It does not matter if the GAL likes the mother or not. The mother can do most anything short of murdering her children and the worst the GAL will oppose the narrative is to recommend joint custody. Consequently, the mother micromanaged the GAL as if the GAL was her own attorney rather than the children's attorney. She encouraged her posse of older women to antagonize the GAL in court, catching the GAL in the corridors screaming that he/she does not understand what is truly going on. They ridicule the GAL, everything short of threats.

Law Enforcement

The current definition of domestic violence is extremely broad. For the most part, across the country, domestic abuse is defined as any intentional and unlawful infliction of physical harm, bodily injury, assault, or the intentional and unlawful infliction of the fear of imminent physical harm, bodily injury, or assault between family or household members. Also included is any criminal sexual act, committed against a family or household member by another family or household member. Claiming fear of physical or sexual harm is impossible to combat. It is an accusation that no one throughout the process will ever require the accusing mother to defend. It is the mother's word against the fathers. And once this pandora's box has been opened, it cannot be closed. The genie cannot be placed back within the lamp. Investigations into the mother's allegations will only be able to state that abuse is or is not indicated, but never that it did not occur.

When the mother makes an allegation, law enforcement will become aware of the accusation and become involved within CPS' investigation, the Child Advocacy Center's forensic interviews, medical examinations, etc. The mother can visit her county's Chief Magistrate, or equivalent, and petition them to arrest the father and serve a protection from abuse order. If the father comes within so many feet of the mother following the protection from abuse order, then law enforcement will arrest him and all of the mother's allegations are conveniently found plausible, case shut, she gets sole custody and the family money.

The mother with the agenda will often have called the police several times well in advance of her heavy hitting allegations. The mother can call 911 for help claiming the father has packed her bags and is demanding her to leave. When the police arrive, they will see the bags, and dismiss anything he has to say. While they take the mother's report, the mother will use this opportunity to make accusations of previous physical abuses. The old, packed bags call is a timeless one that makes him look toxic with a false belief of his male superiority. The mother also antagonized the father by kicking him, smacking him, things that will not leave a mark, but should get him to react possibly putting his hands on her. If he does not take the bait and chooses to call the police on her for help, she can claim he was blocking her from trying to get away, and that he uses the system to control and threaten her. She takes advantage of the law labelling her as the weaker vessel throughout this process. In the eyes of the legal system the father is not permitted to be afraid of the mother.

Counsellors
The mother will probably use many counsellors throughout the

whole situation for herself. The children will have counsellors at the school, and likely a court appointed counsellor as well. The judge will appoint a conflict counsellor for the mother and father. The mother with an agenda has already shopped for counsellors and long begun during the marriage talking to a counselor to create a picture of unhappiness, emotional abuse, etc. She has already established a foundation that she will point to later. The mother can search for counsellors the way she did while interviewing for the right attorney.

The mother had her child see a counsellor at the school. This is especially beneficial during the protection from abuse order. The mother briefed the counsellor, principal, teachers, on the allegations. Not many people will consider anyone would make such allegations maliciously so during this shocking period of losing their father any change in behavior in the child will be noted and documented supportive of the agenda.

In the event the judge orders the mother and father to have psychological evaluations done, the mother needed to be aware of some of the diagnoses that could appear. The judge will likely appoint a specific psychiatrist to perform the psych evals. As with each person that is court appointed, they will be made aware what the narrative is that the judge is desiring. The psych eval consists of tests that will clearly reveal any issues the mother or father has. The psychiatrist will have to make their diagnosis based on the tests, but the severity of which diagnosis the psychiatrist selects is open to discretion. Discretion can be argued to be nothing more than personal opinion, providing a means to dismantle any unfavorable diagnosis the mother received.

If the psychiatrist does find something that must be diagnosed, then the mother and her attorneys must learn everything there is to know about the diagnosis so that they can help the judge downplay the significance of the diagnosis. The mother's attorneys should be prepared to attack the psychiatrist's experience, opinion, and twist the trauma of the mother believing her child has been abused into justifying the psychiatrist making a personal opinion on the mother.

Child Advocacy Center (CAC.)

The Child Advocacy Center, or CAC, is the office that focuses on prevention and intervention of child abuse. The Child Advocacy Center will conduct the forensic interviews. The CAC has a matrix of organizations to execute a well-defined process of investigating the accusations. The multidisciplinary team generally consists of Child Protective Services, Law Enforcement, Forensic Interview Services, Medical Services, Mental Health Services, the District Attorney's Office, and Family and Victim Advocacy Services. They respond to the allegations and determine through non-invasive physical examinations if the children are safe and arrest any guilty abusers.

The forensic interview is a recorded meeting with the child to get information about a possible event that the child experienced or witnessed. The information provided by the child will be instructive in a criminal investigation and corroborate, or refute, allegations or suspicions of abuse. The interview provides a safe, neutral environment, that will allow the child to provide as many details as possible without introducing any specific information from the interviewer. At times the interviewer will ask open-ended questions, or prompts, that encourages the child to respond in further detail.

Often interviewers invite the children to draw during the interview. Drawing encourages them to share more information. The interviewer must gain rapport with the child by beginning slow, gaining basic knowledge, family names, hobbies, friends' names, etc. They will then lead the child into more open-ended questions, then into some specific questions based upon what the child can handle. The purpose of non-leading questions is to help encourage the child to give details in their own words of the abuse. Interviewers should be good at using encouraging words, but not strong responses that influence in any way while the child is talking. Proper moments of silence provide a child with time to gather their thoughts.

CACs are multidisciplined centers whose function is to assure safety and minimize trauma to the children, throughout the investigation of alleged physical and sexual abuses. The medical exams, and forensic interviews, are carried out in child friendly environments, by experienced professionals. The forensic interview is a single session meeting that is recorded and watched real time by other members of the multidisciplinary team such as prosecutors, CAC attorneys, victim advocates, and others. These members watch via live stream to reduce number of interviews and stressors on the child. These mothers never saw their judge permit these interviews into the trial, due to protection of the child's privacy rights.

Private Investigators

There are many reasons for the mother to hire a private investigator, PI. She will want to have a PI search for proof the father is hiding assets, gambling, having affairs, abusing alcohol, using drugs, or any other various illegal activities. Private Investigators are professionals at secretly looking for these things and will provide her with solid proof to use in her case against her husband. They are trained and experienced at following the father without being detected. They will be able to capture photos and videos that can be used in trial. And while she is divorcing the father she will have control of the finances, so he will be the one paying for it to be used against himself.

As with every other tool she has been using through this process, she will want to interview several PI's. She should ask her attorney, old church ladies, ladies she befriended in the shelter for recommended PI's. Do they know of PI's that would help create situations that would support her narrative? She will ask if they can help her find one that will do the things she is wanting done to create something beneficial for her case. Call a few, and schedule consultations. At the consultations she discusses her case, and what she wanted them to find on the father. The consultation may be free, or not, but following this consultation they will not be able to provide services to the father, due to being conflicted out, otherwise known as now having a conflict of interest.

As with everyone else she asks the private investigators for their resumes. The mother verified if they are licensed, what their education is in, as well as different types of certifications. She is also interested in what kinds of cases they have had experience with? How open are they to spinning ideas to fit her allegations, especially if they would testify in trial to it as well. She also read online reviews from their previous clients. The more negative the review is by the one the PI was tracking, the better. Just like with her attorney, she is not looking for a friend. She wants to hire a bulldog that will make things happen.

The mother is crystal clear with the Private Investigator on what she wants. She tasks them with looking for any reason to support the father losing all custody of his children. She has the Private Investigator interview people that see the father with his children, such as: neighbors, teachers, counsellors, and others that may have a regular interaction with them. As they follow him, and watch his home, they can look for the use of alcohol, drugs, affairs, cleanliness of the home, availability of food, etc. The mother also requests that the PI leave indicators around the father's residence to let him know he is being watched. She wants him to talk about being followed, etc. This will allow her attorneys and the judge to say he is paranoid.

Support

Shelter

Shelters are safe places provided for women and children in need of a place to stay while they escape their abuser. Once the mother went to the emergency room and claimed the first abuse allegation, they introduced her to a Child Protective Services representative. This representative offered to the mother a shelter, as well as developed a safety plan for the mother and her children. Once she was at the shelter, she discovered Domestic Violence Support Groups and other means of support for her use. There will be telephone support hotlines that are available around the clock, as well as online tools. Management at the shelter gave her pamphlets and tell her of hotlines available for women all times of the day and night for anything from questions to ongoing emergency situations. She met victims at the shelter. She befriended these ladies to learn the ins and outs of working the system to its fullest potential. The mother was ever careful to never say she was suicidal, but often left people wondering if she was considering it due to the stress and trauma. The mother straddled that fence so that everyone was afraid to confront her from fear of pushing her over the edge.

Every shelter is not set up to be able to provide every service that she may be in need of. However, every shelter will have someone that can help her locate where to get assistance with each particular matter that they cannot assist her with. There are seven main services that shelters can provide her assistance with, and each of those have additional services within themselves.

Seven Main Services a Shelter can help provide:
1. Emergency services. In emergency situations, these shelters offer services with crisis intervention, shelter, confidential shelter location, case management, food and clothing, safety plan development and implementation, education on domestic violence, and even emergency cell phones.
2. Legal services and financial services, such as:
   a. assistance with orders of protection
   b. attorney referral for protection orders
   c. attorney referral for criminal cases
   d. attorney referral for family court
   e. court accompaniment/advocacy
   f. expert testimony
   g. legal resource planning
   h. immigrant services; and
3. Financial Services.
   a. in-shelter financial assistance
   b. financial empowerment training
4. Counseling services.

      a. shelter resident counseling
      b. non-resident counseling
      c. peer support groups
      d. counseling for friends and family, and
      e. substance abuse counseling

5. Housing services.
      a. alternative housing counseling and transportation.

6. Support services.
      a. goal planning assistance
      b. job skills training
      c. resource and referrals, and
      d. medical accompaniment

7. Tutoring services for children and be a school liaison.

Shelters also provide education to the community on domestic violence through workshops.

She is a mother in severe distress. Appearances are critical. She made herself appear distraught at times to the point she seemed incapable of making any improvements in her life.

She visited websites such as childwelfare.gov and make phone calls to the Child help National Child Abuse Hotline at 1-800-4-A-Child (1-800-422-4453) to speak with professional crisis counselors 24 hours a day, 7 days a week. These calls are completely confidential, never discussed in the trials, and therefore allow her to ask any question she may have, as well as providing her information and referrals to thousands of emergency, social service, and support resources. These conversations provide learning opportunities of what lines work and which ones do not.

School

The school provides the mother with several different mandatory reporters she can choose from: teachers, principals, nurse, counsellors, and sometimes a law enforcement officer dedicated to the school. These individuals see the mother's child every day of school. Typically, the mother is the adult point of contact for the school to discuss and matters concerning the child. The mother became involved with the parent teacher organization, volunteered when the school requested help for activities, etc. The mother ensured she had face time with the teachers and began dropping hints of issues at home and how resilient her child is, etc. She was careful during this time to never go so far as to require a mandatory reporter to file a report. She utilized that time to build repertoire with the school officials.

Some mothers wisely begin by making their first allegation with one of the mandatory reporters at the school. They made the allegation with either the nurse, the teacher, or a counsellor to initiate the first investigation for the foundation of the Protection From Abuse order that she immediately pursues thereafter. The reporters, as required, quickly reported it to Child Protective Services. However, other mothers have made their first allegation elsewhere, such as with the emergency room. Either path selected, the mothers immediately share the accusations with the school. Mothers normally meet the principal and counsellor in person, providing them with a hardcopy of the protection from abuse order showing that the court has ordered a restraining order against the father due to an accusation of sexual abuse.

School teachers are usually so very supportive that upon hearing the allegation that they often provide the mother with their personal phone numbers asking the mother to call and text them at any hour of the day so they can help in any way possible. The mother knew the value of these phone numbers and saved them for future use. The mother knew to not overwhelm any one mandatory reporter, therefore when the mother decides to pull the teacher off the bench into play, she frantically texted the teacher to create chaos and worry for the teacher of the child's safety. In this manner the teacher becomes the one talking with the counsellor and the principal, providing awareness without making the principal and counsellor seeing the mother's face too often. The more individuals that are panicked, the stronger the support system for the mother. The larger the support system, the more attention the court must place on the matter.

The Mother's Attorney

The mother will interact with many attorneys throughout this adventure. She began by vetting attorneys before she turned loose her allegation. The mother is in total control of her vessel. By strategically navigating these waters, the court orders the father to pay for her attorneys. Knowing that he will be required to pay, she interviewed multiple prestigious attorneys for one of whom she could micromanage. For finding attorneys to interview, she questioned and listened to old church ladies, as well as the women she met in the shelter. She used the internet to read attorney reviews. She took notice on which attorneys have a resume of work with child sex crimes. She met with at least 5 of the top 10 attorneys in her area for consultations. Due to the nature of the allegations, these consultations are typically free so that the alleged abuser is not made prematurely aware.

- Attorney Interviews – listed below are some basic questions the mother asked:
    - how long have they practiced law
    - do they have any experience with a divorce involving allegations of sexually abusing minor children
    - what is their approach to holding negotiations/ mediations
    - ask to see a template of the interrogatories and discovery they will request on her behalf so that she can add and revise to tailor it case specific
    - how many people within their firm will also be working on her case and see their resumes
    - what is the turnover rate like in their firm
    - what is their win loss ration with trials
    - how many times they have practiced in the courthouse that has jurisdiction of the mother's divorce
    - how many times have they been accused of

    attorney misconduct
- are there any conflicts of interest
- will they allow her to review every motion and attorney to attorney discussion they have?

The mother searched for an attorney that would work closely with her and allow her to micromanage her case. Experienced attorneys will immediately see that the mother will do anything to win, and to many attorneys a highly motivated client is intriguing. However, every individual has a time limit to how long they are willing to have their every move micromanaged.

Church

Churches are intended to be a safe place where people can love, teach, reach, learn, have fellowship, and care for one another in their community. Unfortunately, most churches are nothing more than social hours held without serving strong liquor. Many people use church as a place to network and gain better job opportunities, learn the latest gossip within their communities, and find likeminded individuals. Churches are full of hurt people. Religion is one of the best, if not the best, tools a mother can use to gain unwavering support.

The mother visited multiple churches taking full advantage of economies of scale. She knew that the larger the net she cast the larger her catch would be. There is no bag limit, and always an open season for men and women seeking someone to listen to them at church, and to have someone new they can feel like they are helping. She charismatically shared her story with whomever would listen to her at the churches to gain immediate sympathy allowing her to skip the normal breaking in phase most people must go through to reach invitations to the pastors' homes. Many churches, like the justice system, believe at their core that the woman is the weaker vessel, when it is convenient. They are programmed to believe anything a lady in distress tells them without ever entertaining a word with the accused father before they participate in his total excommunication. She isolates him at every opportunity, within every environment. His complete isolation is critical for a fragile identity to fall apart.

In the presence of the congregation the mother dramatically orchestrates an emotional prayer. The more emotional she was, the more the people wanted to meet her and help her. The congregation believed they felt the spirit emanating from her. The mother placed her pride to the side, playing up to the preachers about being the weaker vessel. She came across broken, distraught, saddened, worried, etc. She informed the pastor and their security to look for a wild, violent, crazed man wanting to get his hands on her or her children. She shared with them a financial situation where the man had taken all of the money and she did not know how she was going to make ends meet to take care of her children. The churches eagerly donate money to her, each church eagerly donating to her that she visits to share a story of sexually abused children at the hands of a violent crazed man. The church is prime hunting grounds to destroy the father's reputation in the community. This in turn further isolated him. The mother in turn grows her network exponentially providing future opportunities in multiple different areas.

Sugar Daddies

Sugar daddies in this summary is not age restrictive. Here, they are the men that trip over themselves to help a damsel in distress. The mother finds it easy to rehearse her agenda in real time with these preachers, deacons, youth ministers, teachers, principals, any of the men that are within her circles. Sugar daddies are genetically programmed with the need to save a woman asking for help. Sugar daddies are first and foremost just men, they feel good when they feel needed. She gives them attention and gives them tasks they can help her with and they are simply her's to manipulate. She makes it easy for them to talk with her. She approaches them initiating conversations and makes them think they are unique and special. Many of them have been married for decades. When is the last time someone giggled at their jokes, or complimented the way their lips purse when he is deep in concentration? As they help her and listen to her story she finds ways to thank them. Can a damsel in distress have too many useful men feeling like they are her knights in shining armor ready to defeat the dark dragon haunting her and her children?

Now that she has this entourage of sugar daddies, she gets to choose which task each one needs to vanquish for her. Some of them she will want to hold in reserve due to what and when they have that can best serve her. Some she will be able to micromanage as they grovel at her feet. Some will become needy. Some will likely even be creepy, but useful.

She probes them for who they know, how much influence they have and where. Do they know people within the courthouse that can listen to anything concerning her case? Do they have a cousin that works for an organization that she would like to work at? Do they have a niece that works for Child Protective Services? Do they work in the father's organization?

Some of the sugar daddies will be handymen, mechanics, and good with their hands. Some can get her whatever substances she may need to without anyone finding out. Perhaps some are private investigators that can provide her services at a discount, or even free. Some will be intimately familiar with the corrections' treatment of child predators and choose to be the savior of her and her children. She has them taking care of all the work around her house, maintaining her car, and servicing any other need she wants them to perform.

Most of the sugar daddies will annoy the mother. The mother's belief system is built upon the fact that there is not one situation where she needs a man but having a large support system is paramount to her agenda. She will have moments of severe frustration where she is shaken to her core having to continue acting like these men are her saviors. But her support grows the more she is seen as the weaker vessel, the delicate damsel in distress. We must not forget that men are here for our use.

Sugar Mamas

As there are sugar daddies, there are also what we will simply call sugar mamas. These are the lonely older women seeking attention at churches. Many of them having issues of their own and suffering from depression, loneliness, confidence. They can be found using churches as a social hour to gain favor, advantages, a manufactured purpose. They will approach the new kid on the block, the mother, and introduce her to other sugar mamas. The mother shares her allegations and the older women immediately welcome her into their fold serving her indefinitely. The mother finds that a good number of these women have used the system to take everything away from their ex-husbands. They share their experiences and the mother soaks them up like a sponge. She is initiated into a group that greases any tracks that lie before her. We are never alone, we just have to look for our sisters in this cause for justice against the suppression.

The connections grow strong and intense with these sugar mamas, sharing experiences through the nights in one another's tender care. Through laughter and tears they feed off one another's plots and schemes. Her sugar mamas will compete for who gets to spend the most time with the mother. They pay for food, entertainment, trips, clothes, anything to share their time helping the mother. They provide the mother with beneficial connections, attorneys, counsellors, etc. They watch her children for her and voluntarily help coach her children when they feel the system is not getting it right. The older women's experiences already teaching them the system does not issue anything more than a verbal warning to stop coaching to the mother or the mother's entourage. Most of these sugar mama's were around when the term malicious mother syndrome was laughed out of the court and renamed parental alienation to that could be rightfully directed at the father as another means to grant sole custody to the mother. Sugar mamas will do anything for the mother if she makes them feel like someone wants them and allows them to be a part of destroying a man.

Sugar mamas will encourage the mother to have an interest in hobbies, a job, going back to school, changing her hair, whatever they think will help her heal and get through this terrible time in her life. During a divorce process, especially one consisting of child sexual abuse allegations, the mother has no reason to work. The mother used her extra time to coach her children. She did what she could to alienate them from their father, his family, and anyone else that was still in his corner. She interferes with any time they could have with their father. She speaks negatively about the father and his friends. She rewards her children for saying bad things about their father. She uses corporal punishment to maintain fear within the hearts of her children. She knows, and the sugar mama's remind her, that the justice system encourages a mother to utilize corporal punishment as long as no bones are broken. Many child protective services even permitting welts and bruises left by the mother using a stick to hurt her child, as long as she denies it but says within her cultural upbringing it is permitted. Parental alienation is when one parent uses all tactics at their disposal to attempt to, or often succeed, at causing the children to dislike and distrust the other parent. And the sugar mamas help her because they know they must do what it takes to put the father in prison.

The Judge

These mothers found that the judge is there to listen to what facts support the narrative and prevent those that do not. They are supposed to base this narrative on what is best for all parties involved in the divorce. The judge is going to listen to the subject matter experts' reports on each parent's ability to meet the needs of the children; the relationship between the children and each parent; which parent is attempting to alienate their children from the other; history of abuse or neglect especially all allegations made by the mother; stability of each parent; each parent's living situation; distance parents live from one another; and possibly consider the children's preference and why.

The mother knows that at the very least she will receive joint custody of the children, half of the assets, the house, the best car, the dogs, alimony, child support, etc. But this is not good enough, the mother deserves it all. So the mother provided the judge with what she could to support the court's narrative that the man should hand over everything to the mother, including all his time with the children. The mother crafted his fall, to get it all. Whenever a mother claims abuse, the court will assist in creating or supporting obstacles for the man to try and navigate through, to hopefully trigger him into a negative outburst that can then be used against him.

Immediately after the judge issued the PFA, the mother filed for divorce. By the mother being the one to file for divorce first, the father is permanently labelled the defendant through the divorce and custody process. The judge will issue a pendente lite order, that will require him to continue paying all expenses for the mother and her children, home, car, utilities, insurances, as well as his new residence and living expenses. Most men will make things very easy at this point when he can no longer see his children and has been kicked out of his home. He may very well act out in a negative manner trying to survive under this pressure and growing isolation due to the nature of the allegations. Whatever negative reaction he has, whether it is breaking the no contact restraining order within the PFA, getting a DUI, getting into a scuffle somewhere, having a wreck, and unfortunately sometimes committing suicide, it will allow the judge to claim the accusations are plausible resulting in the mother receiving sole custody, and all assets as he is led to prison. If he is found guilty for sexually abusing his children the mother will get absolutely everything. If he commits suicide the mother will also get everything. If he runs, well, that is abandonment and the mother still likely gets everything. How can she lose when the judge will enable every one of her actions? For the sole purpose of advancing the desired outcome of the mother receiving sole custody, the judge will often join the mother's attorney in directly questioning the father in the trial.

The judge also makes any necessary rulings on contempt of court. In divorce court, contempt of court primarily applies only to the man. In the event the mother is ever confronted on any of her contempt of court infractions, the judge only wants to hear her say she was confused and nothing further will be said. The orders may include statements such as both the mother and father shall remain living in a specific county; or neither parent is permitted to carry the child outside of this certain area, etc. These statements are 'shall do' directives to the father, and seemingly on average 'should to' for the mother. Contempt of court is so very useful in the narrative for the mother to get sole custody. If the father breaks a court order he will be found in contempt of court, be jailed, face financial penalties, and perhaps even lose his job.

The Opposition

The Father's Attorney

The father will have his own divorce and custody attorney, and depending on the extent of the mother's allegations, he likely will have had to hire a criminal defense attorney. The mother's attorneys will interact with his attorneys. Nearly every pendente lite order directs the father to pay for all of the mother's legal fees through the divorce, especially if the mother was a stay-at-home mother when she filed for divorce. The more legal fees the mother creates for her attorneys and his, the further in debt the father sinks, which increases the likelihood of him having a negative outburst under the intense pressure being placed on him.

The father's attorneys very rarely have any interaction with the mother. They only engage the mother to question her at depositions and trials. If the mother represents herself pro se, they will occasionally be required to engage the mother as opposing counsel.

The Father

The mothers describe the father with the accusations detailed throughout this book. Every mother has her unique difficulty that only she can specifically define. As you read through this book, and see what they went through to protect their children, you will be encouraged and experience personal images appearing within your mind's eye. Stay strong my sister.

CHAPTER 2 –
CROSSING THE
RUBICON

Now that we have properly introduced the entities typically involved with such allegations, let us discuss some options that the mother experienced in her journey. She had decided it was long past time to get the father out of the picture. She had considered how easy it would be to just murder him, but the risk was too high. Being a mother in America provides many more fruitful options with near zero risk to get him out of her life forever. So she decided to put him in prison for the rest of his life. She knew she would never have to cooperate with him if she made allegations of a child sex allegation. She knew the current American justice system, this golden age for mothers, would enable her throughout her endeavor, with the highest likelihood of zero accountability.

First and foremost, she developed a pre-divorce checklist. If the father has a checklist, the mother and her attorney should use this to label him as controlling, financially abusive, manipulative, and trying to hide marital assets from the mother. The judge will consider it wisdom, and being a nurturing mother for the mother to develop and follow a pre-divorce checklist to ensure nothing is missed. The following list is not complete and needs to be tailored for each unique case.

Example of a Pre-Divorce Checklist
☐Open a checking account and a savings account in her name

alone in a different bank. Begin shifting funds into her new personal accounts. The court system encourages the mother to have this as an "emergency fund."

☐ Open a credit card in her name alone.

☐ List all current marital assets and debts.

☐ List assets that belonged to her before the marriage, premarital assets.

☐ List items of his that she wants to claim were hers before the marriage. If he does happen to present some proof that something she claims was his before marriage, then all she has to say is she was confused. No one will questions her any further.

☐ Make copies of current mortgage bill, utilities bill, health insurance policy, phone, internet, cable, auto notes and insurance,

☐ Provide copies of predivorce quality of life bills such as, salon, masseuse, chiropractor, sauna, pool membership, etc. Feel free to embellish. Who keeps copies of all receipts, right?

☐ Copy of his social security card.

☐ Copy of his driver's license.

☐ Copy of his pistol permit, hunting license, fishing license.

☐ Copies of anything pertaining to his place of employment.

☐ Copies of at least the past three years of tax returns.

☐ Attain as many of his passwords to apps, websites, accounts, etc. Have him use her computer well in advance of her allegations of sexual abuse. He will likely choose the options for her computer to remember his passwords to his different apps and websites. Make sure she and he have separate social media accounts so that she can periodically write messages from his account to hers. Then she is sure to send multiple messages to him so that he does not scroll up and look for any previous messages. He will not notice. Begin creating as much shade as possible. It will likely be useless in court, but it will be read and create a negative image of the father. As soon as she does make the allegation of sexual abuse ensure she takes her computer with her and change his passwords. Connect these apps and websites of his account to a new email address she creates for herself.

☐ Go to post office and get a post office box.

☐ At the post office apply to have all mail forwarded to a trusted person, or her new PO Box.

☐ Attain copies, or make notes, of any information pertaining to the assets of his parents, siblings, and close friends. She will want to be aware of everything anyone owns that may stand by his side through her allegations. She must be prepared to drain their life savings through multiple allegations. She is preparing for war, and scorched earth. She is crossing the Rubicon.

☐ Interview a minimum of three attorneys, or at least create a list of questions to go over with at least three attorneys before she makes her allegation that begins the Protection from Abuse and Divorce process. She wants to find an attorney that is a beast, a jerk, yet malleable to her desires. She is searching for an attorney open to being micromanaged through this process. Discuss her plans with them during official consultations and listen carefully to their reactions and responses. The nature of the allegation will gain influence with acquiring many quality attorneys that do not yet realize her agenda.

She tried everything she could to create reactions from him that would allow her to build an actual history of abuse leading up to her main allegation. She bombarded him with endless fault finding and finger pointing. She belittled him in public. She micromanaged his every move keeping him on a short leash. She over dramatized everything. She isolated him from his friends and family through ultimatums. It is possible he never did confront her, no matter how hard she tried to antagonize him into a confrontation she could use against him. It is of very little importance. No factual abuse is required for her allegation of child sexual abuse.

As a result of the mother's allegations, she observes the people in his life fell into three categories.

1. The first category, which is where most of his relationships fell into were people that permanently cease all contact with him and believe the mother without ever asking him a single question. They will not speak to him. They do not want his side of the story.

2. The second category, which were more of his closer relationships fell into were people that never believe her allegations but permanently cease all contact with him without ever asking him a single question. They do not want to be seen speaking to someone accused of such an allegation.

3. The third category, these people will see through the mother's agenda. These people will not abandon the father and his children. Many of them have survived similar situations themselves. They have seen the children with their father through the years. Some of them have known the father for decades. They will stand with the father against her agenda. The mother will seek ways to divide and conquer these individuals. There will be many opportunities that reveal themselves for her to deplete this group through the long process. The mother will use her charisma, connections, etc. to encourage this group to distance themselves from the situation. She does not seek to win this group over into her corner, only to cause them to abandon the father.

The law of nature says that the female is attracted to the male that can provide the most benefit to her, the most resources. The demands she placed on the father has stolen his youth and handicapped his ability to gather more resources. She has decided it is time to move on. She focused on her image. She fine tuned it into what she needed to make her next catch, someone that deserved her.

She is the only one that can decide how extensive her first allegation will be. She knows that court system will need to hear something like he tickled his child's privates, or that he raped his children while she was gone. Did the mother choose the slower approach, building up to the rape accusation after she has the pediatrician probe her child for chlamydia? Proper planning prevents poor performance. Each step of the process can literally be programmed into a Gantt chart with start and end dates to help her stay on target. She knows she should never trust that she will remember how and when to react, so she uses google calendar to set up reminders for her next allegations in advance.

The Trip

It is now go time. She pulls the trigger, figuratively. She plans a trip with a friend, taking all children except a daughter, preferably under the age of 5. As soon as she and the friend leave she begins discussing how terrible her life is and that she needs someone to help her find a way out. She cries on this friend's shoulder. She uses the weaker vessel persona to her advantage. She claims a history of previous abuses saying that she stayed for the children, and that the father kept promising to stop this or that.

On the second or third night of the trip while the two are creating ideas on ways to make him pay for all of the horrible things he has done to her, she begins saying things about him being alone with her daughter. They become so worked up that they begin saying they do not know who this man is. She says she does not know what he is capable of. She says he has sick fetishes and has tried to force her to do this or that.

Late into the evening one of them declares they must return home immediately. They rush home in the middle of the night. She is defining the first battle. She is going to blindside him creating a controlled chaos with this friend to observe anything that could be twisted for the coming allegation. All she needs for her allegation is to say they observed a difference in the child's behavior. She creates a tactical advantage of speed and spontaneity.

The ideal thing to do at this point would be for the mother to take the child immediately to the emergency room and make the allegation. However, many mothers continue to stall wanting to get every detail perfected beforehand. So the next day she and the friend begin calling and interviewing different attorneys to find the right one. She takes her child to the emergency room to craft his fall, to get it all.

Initial Allegation

The mother is the only one that can decide if she claims sexual abuse, or reports concerns of her child behaving differently with implied sexual abuse concerns. She is defining her total victory, and a life time prison sentence for her husband. This is all or nothing. So she and a friend take her child to the emergency room. Once she is there she requests that the emergency room check her child to see what is wrong, because she is behaving differently after staying alone for a night or two with her abusive father.

Once at the emergency room, one or more of the following is what she reported to CPS or Law Enforcement:

- Neglect:
    - Physical Neglect is when a parent or caretaker of the child does not provide the basic survival needs to the child such as food, shelter, their cleanliness, or if they have access to a doctor or dentist.
    - Educational Neglect happens when the parent or caretaker of the child does not enroll the child into their mandatory school, nor provide homeschool need to the child.
    - Medical Neglect is when the parent of caretaker does not provide the child access to a doctor or dentist to correct or prevent sickness or other health care needs of the child.

- ○ Chronic Neglect is when the parent or caretaker of the child continues to neglect the child with no sign of stopping without intervention for the child to get proper care when and where needed.
- Description of the incidents of physical abuse done to the mother and/or her child(ren.) When and where the incident(s) occurred.
- Description of the incidents of sexual abuse done to her and/or her child(ren.) When and where the incident(s) occurred. There is no witness required, only a claim that the mother has noticed a change in the child(ren)'s behavior. Some accusations can include: the child has suddenly become afraid to be around the father; the child will no longer enter a certain room; the child suddenly has mature knowledge of sexual matters; etc. These can be completely unprovable claims. This begins the spinning of a web, a snowball at the top of a hill gently being pushed to begin rolling down the hill growing and growing as it gathers speed. She set back and watched the system do the rest for her.
- The justice system respects accusations of emotional abuse only when made by the woman. Emotional abuse to children occurs when a parent or one of their caretakers hurts a child's emotional development or sense of self-worth through not loving them, never allowing them to be good enough. This person will usually threaten the child, criticize them, never accept them, nor love them. Behavioral changes the mother may have observed are: bed wetting, sudden withdrawal or aggression, and even attention seeking. There are some women that make accusations of bed wetting that pour actual urine, coffee, or tea onto their mattresses creating what appears to be urine stains to support their accusations. No one will ever do a DNA test on it, so it does not matter whose urine it is, or whether it is tea or

coffee.

Once a child is taken to the Emergency Room (ER) and claims of abuse made, the mother and child(ren) are connected with a social worker and law enforcement. The social worker will create a safety plan for her and her children and suggest a shelter for them. While in the shelter the mother will typically receive guidance to file a Protection From Abuse Order (PFA.) The PFA will have law enforcement remove the father from the home. Within the shelter are other women that have gone through many abuses or have experience working the system, so saw them as oracles. She listens intently to their experiences. She shares her story and learned which questions it is they ask her and what response returned the best reaction. The mother was in rehearsal. She learned when to shed tears, when to pause, and when to show anger. She experimented with her responses, tweaking her style where it was beneficial and had the best return on investment.

The doctors ask her in what ways her child is behaving differently. The mother has many options to choose from here, but she can simply say she is suddenly and unexplainably scared of me; she shies away from her dad now; she is suddenly depressed; she will not calm down, etc. The mother can be as creative as she wants to be, many details or not. No one will ever be able to disprove her accusations. CPS investigation can only determine abuse is indicated or not indicated. Most mothers are never held accountable for their accusations. The nurse and the doctor that check the child will be trained and experienced with child victims of physical and sexual abuse and be looking for signs of abuse to proceed with their initial medical investigation. They will share their findings with law enforcement on whether there are indicators that some form of abuse has possibly occurred, or if they have found no indicators.

Her goal at the emergency room is to get a doctor to say that some form of abuse or neglect has possibly occurred to her child(ren) while she was away and the child was alone with their father. She keeps the definition of child abuse in mind when she is making her accusations. It must be something that has recently occurred, or failed to occur on the part of a parent or a caretaker, which results in death, serious physical or emotional harm, sexual abuse or exploitation. She frames her accusations within these parameters. The emergency room staff will direct the mother to a social services representative that will offer her a place at a shelter. On leaving the emergency room the mother takes her children to stay in one of the nearby shelters.

Shelter

After the emergency room doctors and staff finish analyzing the child and documenting the mother's concerns, they will direct the mother to a social services representative that will offer her a place at a shelter. To maintain the facade, she will take her children to the shelter. When she arrives at the shelter she meets several people that work there in a social worker capacity, as well as other women in need of a safe place to stay. The mother describes in detail all the allegations she is casting about her husband to the shelter manager, and shelter counsellor. While at the shelter the staff and other women within the shelter will help her to acquire a protection from abuse order, PFA. The PFA will have law enforcement remove her husband from the home so that she and her children can return home.

The mother built relationships with the other women in the shelter. She knew it was in her best interest to make these women believe she cared about them so that they would be encouraged to share their stories with her. She would use their experiences to advance her own objectives. Some of them have very likely been through the system numerous times and will hold a wealth of information she would benefit from. She observed what it is within their stories that bring someone else to tears or anger. The mother knows that her creativity creates advantage. Her timing of pressing forward, or withdrawing, will be critically influential. Conflict creates change and change creates opportunities she can take advantage of. Within the American justice system it is the damsel in distress' war to lose.

Protection From Abuse Order

The shelter will advise the mother on where to go, as well as who to talk to, for getting an ex parte Protection From Abuse (PFA) order for her minor children from the local county Circuit Court. The PFA is a document signed by a judge directing the alleged abuser to cease all abuse or face dire consequences. The mother's attorney will advise her, or congratulate her, for getting a protection order because of the strategic advantages this tool provides in the divorce and custody battle ahead. They are easy to get, and require no evidence of alleged fear or abuse, only accusations. All that is required is for the mother to go before a judge and claim she is in fear for her or her child(ren)'s safety. She can claim any combination of physical abuse or sexual abuse with no evidence required. She claims he has guns, or that she has reason to believe he has gotten a gun from a friend. She will check some of the boxes asking what weapons have been involved from a suggested list of: firearms, knives, hands, feet, fist, other and if the weapon(s) are still at the property. With one, or a combination, of these small statements the court will enter an order on an emergency basis restraining her husband from his children, his home, and locking all finances down for weeks, and up to several months, until the hearing can be scheduled. This temporary order will remain in affect until the PFA hearing.

Within the PFA she writes that the father, now the defendant, cannot come within 300 feet, and check the boxes that this includes places of work and the children's school. She sends this PFA to the school for their awareness garnering additional support.

She checks all the boxes that the defendant is prohibited from transferring, concealing, encumbering, otherwise disposing of specified property mutually owned or leased by the parties. The father has now lost his children, his home, and cannot do anything with the family money all while continuing to pay for everything. She checks the box that the PFA Orders the Defendant to pay her attorney's fees and court costs.

She claims the father did one or more of many options provided within the PFA paperwork. Common ones to select are: Made the Plaintiff afraid that the Plaintiff would be seriously injured; tortured or willfully abused the Plaintiff's child(ren); Recklessly engaged in conduct which risked serious injury to the Plaintiff; and Injured the Plaintiff. As she has just spoken with Child Protective Services that morning, or the day before, while she was in the shelter, she makes sure to write in that her husband is currently under investigation by Child Protective Services and the Child Advocacy Center for Sexually abusing his child(ren.)

The form asks her why she is genuinely fearful the defendant will cause further abuse. She writes in that she is concerned for her children's safety because he has also been physically abusive to her in the past, so she is afraid of what he may do. She has been planning and building up to this moment, so over the past few years, she has already made a few calls to law enforcement to report him for something, no matter how minor or authentic. She reports the classic he packed my bags and was going to make me leave story. While it is not necessary to have her children report anything within their interviews, a history of reports the mother had been building influenced the judge from the very beginning as to what the father's character was like without even having to speak to him. The protection order is a tactical silver bullet.

Once the mother has filed the protection order, she visits the chief magistrate and tried to get an arrest warrant for the father based on whatever allegations she has currently opted to pursue. She views each of these interactions with the legal system as marketing meetings where she is trying to sell her story to gain influence and have the father arrested.

When law enforcement receives the PFA they will send a convoy to kick him out of his house. The mother and children then leave the shelter to go home. Now he has abandoned the home, forced or not, abandonment is abandonment for the woman in the justice system. No one will ever want to remove the children from their childhood home. This will be used in her favor greatly affecting custody determinations, child support calculations, and property division in the final divorce and custody orders.

Most men put into this position will provide the mother everything she needs to have him locked up. The father is not permitted to talk to his children, and is kicked out of his home by a small convoy of law enforcement officers due to unforeseen accusations of sexually abusing his children. He will face the most traumatic event of his life. The mother has backed him into a corner with no escape, nor any means to fight back. He either must place his trust in the hands of people he does not know, or lash out. His mind will try to process the trauma. He has no time to waste on trying to heal. He will have to immediately begin trying to heal, or the judge will see him as unfit through his bottled up emotions, which are Post Traumatic Stress Disorder, PTSD. If the father comes inside the distance limit set within the PFA order the mother will call the police and report him immediately. He will be arrested. The mother knows any time she can get him to act out poorly, touch her, contact the children, etc. she only needs to call the police, and they will arrest him immediately. If he disobeys any restraining orders, it will not matter what the mother has alleged, she will have complete victory.

The mother is aware of PTSD, but learning more about it provides her with more options to use against him through the process. The following are examples of what he is now encountering:

- Hopes and dreams he had suddenly disappear.
- He will distance himself from others; and due to the nature of her accusations, he has already been completely isolated. He will learn to distrust people. He will find it nearly impossible to make new friends. He may become detached from society.
- He will find it difficult, or impossible to focus. This will affect his ability to keep a job.

- He will make bad decisions, or not be able to make beneficial decisions.
- His nerves will always be on edge. His instincts will place him in defensive mode constantly. His anxiety will be off the charts. His heart will pound. He will feel shaky.
- Many men in this position cannot sleep well due to dreams, or endless thoughts preventing them from being able to go to sleep. He will either self-medicate, or seek prescriptions for sleeping pills. This provides another tool for her attorneys and judge to use in their narrative against him. This awareness will increase the likelihood of him entering into addictions thinking he can avoid prescriptions that will just be used against him.
- His appetite is going to change. Either not eating enough, or bingeing. This only increases his weariness.
- Any preexisting health problems will likely worsen due to the trauma.
- Depression will likely take root and cause him to further lose interest in any healthy activities and relationships.
- Many will commit suicide just to escape this endless war that they does not allow them to fight back, as they watch their children being used.

Allegations of sexual abuse of children will automatically call for the PFA to be an ex parte PFA. Ex parte means that the alleged abuser is not made aware beforehand, or present for the judge to sign the PFA. The husband will have to hire an attorney, and they will both not know what the mother is going to say or do at the hearing. He will be defenseless.

File Divorce

The person that files divorce first has the advantage of being the plaintiff throughout the divorce process. However, the mother does not need to worry if her husband does file first. Court orders within the divorce order are primarily optional for the woman, and jail time for the husband if he breaks any orders. But it is highly unlikely he will file before the mother can while she is at the shelter because of how he was blindsided. The PFA kicked him out of his home with the reason being the mother accusing him of sexually abusing his child(ren). So the mother quickly filed for divorce before he had time to find an attorney to guide him. Yet it is only a matter of time before the father will begin receiving experienced advice from his attorney.

The mother will file the divorce at the local county Circuit Court with her new attorney hired at the husband's expense. Within the divorce the mother has her attorney state that the defendant has subjected one or more of the minor children to incidents of abuse. There is already in place an Ex Parte Protection from Abuse Order protecting the minor children from the father in the county circuit court. The defendant is therefore accused of not being a fit and proper person to exercise custody of the minor children. The mother's attorney states within the divorce filing that she, the Plaintiff, is the fit and proper person to have primary custody and control of the minor child. She ensures her attorney requests within the petition for divorce that due to the accusations within the PFA that the Honorable Court enter this Court's standing pedente lite order and require the children to remain in the primary care of the plaintiff. The attorney also includes that the order restrict the defendant from having visitation or access to the minor children until the court determines the circumstances under which the father can safely visit with the children.

The mother's attorney needs to state within the petition for divorce that the defendant is able bodied and capable of earning wages with which he can provide for the support and maintenance of the plaintiff, the minor children, and attorney fees. The mother has the attorney include anything that can possibly trigger her husband into a negative reaction. She pushes while the court simultaneously enables and encourages her campaign. The faster he disappears, the easier the case will be and further the cause of eliminating the father.

Damage Outdoor Property at Marital Residence

After the PFA has removed the husband from the marital residence and the mother and her children have returned she will want to damage the home and property. She wants to paint a portrait that he is a demented individual. She expects investigators to begin visiting her and her children at her home, as well as her support group that is about to grow exponentially. The mother is fully engaged in acting the role of a weaker vessel, so visitors are going to assume that all the outdoor upkeep has been the husband's responsibility. The mother poisons large portions of the lawn and shrubs. She gets the dog's paw muddy and smears it all over the door. She throws tools around outside. She creates a sloppy, unkempt outdoor greeting for the visitors. This was the father's domain. Visitors will consequently visualize his character as being off.

Within the home the mother will have toys strewn around. A loving mother encourages her children to play with her toys, and a stressed woman will receive sympathy for not making her children put their toys away at this difficult time. The mother will have the stereotypical housewife chores taken care of, such as dishes and clothes put away. She makes it appear she is on top of all the responsibilities an unemployed housewife could be doing. The mother has collected and poured urine on the mattresses within the home. She pours around three to four puddles on each mattress. She may decide to use coffee rather than urine. She only waned to create the appearance that they are urine stains she has found. No one will perform a DNA test to verify whether it is urine or not.

CPS Investigation and Determination

Once the mother makes her accusation at the emergency room and then at the shelter, the Child Protective Services, CPS, will begin their investigation. The investigation will likely last months before they reach a determination. The Child Advocacy Center, CAC, will conduct forensic interviews. The children will undergo medical screenings. During this time the father will not have access to his children, and possibly be arrested. With him out of the picture the mother can coach her children, alienating them further in his absence. She can use this time to make additional accusations. She remembers creativity creates advantage. She will say the children are feeling safer with their father being kept away and they are beginning to reveal additional things to her that their father did to them. It is not necessary for anyone else to ever hear the children say the things she will claim they reveal to her. Nearly every judge will give her the benefit of the doubt. Who can prove otherwise? The burden of proof lies entirely on the father. Investigators may claim she is coaching her children, and if they ever scold her verbally for coaching her children she can just quietly listen and later calls a telephone support hotline, preferably in the middle of the night claiming everyone is against her and does not understand. She is careful to never tell the hotline counselor that she is considering suicide, but she makes insinuations to appear straddling that fence due to the investigators not seeing the truth. The hotline counselor will not be permitted to testify at any hearing, but they may be able to voice their concerns to the judge who will place their thumb on anyone questioning the mother's intentions and actions. Investigators may reveal that the mother is lying, but the judge will ensure that no one will ever be able to say that the children are not making the accusations to only their mother.

Child Protective Services, CPS, begins the process of their investigation with an Initial Assessment, or investigation, to determine whether the child(ren) are in imminent danger, and if there is risk of future abuse. The judge will always lean on the side of caution. The judge will state that the full investigation is not complete, therefore the children's safety is not guaranteed, and further restrict the father's time with his children. It is common for the mother to be able to keep the children from seeing their father for years with these caliber of allegations. Through the long period of time that the children have no contact with their father the mother works at instilling a fear of their father into them. Only the mother can determine how quickly or slowly her approach will be with working on this alienation.

CPS will receive the information from the mother, the reporter. Then they will determine if the reported abuse meets the statutory definition for abuse or neglect. Once CPS determines if the report meets the guidelines for moving forward, they will assess what the response for the child(ren) must be. During this process CPS will provide support and encouragement to the reporting person and reassure the reporter that CPS' purpose is to protect children and make families stronger through actions, education, and preventing abuse or neglect. CPS will be sensitive to the mother's portrayed fear of coming forward. Through this initial conversation CPS will gather enough information to know what immediate protection the children may need and if law enforcement should be notified. They will gather demographic information; what type, or types of abuse allegedly occurred; information about the parents, the child(ren,) and the whole family. CPS will discuss the report with superiors and law enforcement and decide which steps to take next. CPS will interview the child, the parents, and the accused predator. CPS will observe how the child interacts with parents, siblings, other family members, and other people and locations as applicable.

After CPS gathers information, they will then determine if abuse is indicated, or not indicated. If they find abuse is indicated, then the mother will have made an extremely significant victory. The father will be arrested and face criminal charges of sexually abusing his children. He would face a lifetime prison sentence. The mother will receive sole custody. Most importantly to the mother, she will receive sole possession of all marital possessions.

CHAPTER 3 – REGROUP

Many of the following actual examples occurred with CPS determining abuse as not indicated. Child Protective Services (CPS) and the Child Advocacy Center have investigated the mother's allegations and determined that she is coaching her child(ren.) CPS met with the mother a couple days prior to the PFA hearing. They informed the mother that their investigation is complete, and that their determination is that sexual abuse is not indicated. Many people will advise the mother to remain calm, and quiet. But this is not the time to be calm, nor quiet. The mother continues to use the divorce court's view of the woman being the weaker vessel, and be the frightened caring mother trying to keep her children safe from their abusive father. The investigators got it wrong, so the mother makes more accusations of abuse to CPS. Remember creativity is advantageous. They will be required to investigate all the mother's allegations. She has one of her older church lady friends call CPS and claim that the children have disclosed something to them. As CPS begins a new investigation the mother will have time to regroup.

PFA Hearing

The father has no information other than the PFA document that contains a one line allegation that he is accused of physically and/or sexually abusing his child(ren.) The father will still be in shock. He will have himself convinced that there is some mistake, or someone has lied to the mother to create conflict. An hour before the hearing the mother instructed her attorney to hold a discussion with his attorney. She directs her attorney to tell her husband's attorney that she wants to dismiss the PFA and that she desires reconciliation with him. Her husband has had no communication with her or his children this entire time. He does not understand at all what is happening. As he hears the words reconciliation, the carpet will be completely ripped out from under his feet. His brain will not be able to comprehend anything. The mother has him exactly where she needs him for the negotiations.

When the judge learns from the mother's attorney that she is dismissing the PFA and CPS has found no abuse indicated, the judge will direct the attorneys to set in a room with the plaintiff and defendant to discuss what will go into the pendent lite order through the divorce. The mother's attorney will ask for maximum child support, with the mother and the children to remain in the home, etc. The father will agree with all recommendations for the pendent lite order because he is now hopeful that everything is some sick misunderstanding and that this is somehow temporary. He has just agreed to surrendering the house and all the money without any fight, and as a cherry on top he is held financially responsible for keeping everything status quo for the mother and children until the final order of the divorce. However, do keep in mind, that if the mother does dismiss the PFA, the judge is going to take Child Protective Services' investigation results of no abuse indicated, and say they have no proof of abuse to continue taking the father's constitutional rights of being a father away from him and return to him some non-supervised visitation.

On the other hand, if the mother did not dismiss her PFA charges, then her husband is going to have two options at the hearing. First, he can agree with a restraining order which will last a few years until revisited; or he can continue on to an evidentiary hearing to fight the allegations. For the past month or longer since the convoy of police served him the PFA papers he has been living in his car, a shelter, or with family and friends. These are the few people the mother was unable to isolate him from. She has destroyed his good name in the community, and he is not permitted to even speak to his children. She brutally, but successfully, blindsided him. Regardless of which option he takes at this hearing, he will remain distanced from his children. Most men will spiral if they have even made it this far. The mother does not let up.

The father has learned at this hearing that he has lost his children, assets, and good name. He has learned that a pendente lite order will be signed by the judge requiring him to maintain the status quo of his children and the mother's life. He will have to hang on to a job to be able to pay his bills; his wife's attorney's bill; his own divorce attorney's bill; the rent or lease for his new residence, etc. The legal system knows that most men cannot sustain this for long periods of time and that he will typically become a nonfactor soon enough. The mother takes advantage of this current system tipped heavily in the mother's favor.

Pendente Lite Order

Temporary court orders will be used during the divorce process to determine how things will legally progress until the courts can make their final order dissolving the marriage permanently via the divorce. For the mother these orders are primarily optional, mere suggestions, but provides her with additional firepower to charge her husband with all orders he does not obey. The man will be held in contempt, jailed, if he breaks any directives set forth within the court orders. It can be said with respect to civil court divorce and custody cases that for the mother, the court order is a should. While a court order for the man is a shall.

The court order set forth when the divorce is initially filed is sometimes referred to as a pendente lite order. Sometimes the hearing to get the temporary order can be foregone if the attorneys can offer an agreement to the court to be ordered. If the court does decide on the necessity to hold a hearing to get the temporary order, then the mother follows her attorney's lead. The onus will be on the accused child molester husband to state his case on why he should have access to finances, etc. Dress and act the part of the weaker vessel and the judge will ensure the results are in the mother's favor.

The following are generic items the mother will see in the pendente lite order:

- The order will state clearly that neither party is allowed to sale the marital home until the final divorce order.
- It will decide which party, or parties, can reside in the marital home through the divorce process.
- It will state who gets which vehicle, as well as where the money will come from to pay for the cars' notes.
- The order will list who pays what amount of child support and include calculations, or any standard calculation rule followed, to arrive at the child support amounts.
- It will list what, if any, spousal support allowances are to be clearly paid throughout the divorce process.
- The order will define the child custody and visitation schedules.
- Health insurance responsibilities will be listed as to who is responsible to keep the health insurance covering the children, as well as how coverage will be maintained on the spouse, especially if the mother is a nonworking spouse.
- An order may go as far as to preemptively detail who is responsible to pay for medical expenses not covered by health insurance for the children as well as the spouses.
- An order may contain a no contact, no harassment, clause.
- And the order will likely detail that no party is permitted to sell any valuable assets and marital possessions.
- The father will be directed to maintain status quo the lifestyle the mother and children are accustomed to.

She does not permit legal documents to concern her. While

this blocks the man out of the life he has built, she can conceal income, move funds, spend funds, transfer funds, and push her husband out of any financial matters. If her husband has lasted this long not being able to even speak to his children, and having everything taken away from him, he will encounter an extreme reality check when this legal document comes to his hands. His attorney will explain to him that this order is what he is responsible for over the next couple years until the divorce is completed. Many men will obviously fall apart at the seams upon this long-term realization of having to fund the very agenda set against him. Whatever negative reaction the father chooses, a man six feet under by his own hand, or behind bars for over thirty years, the mother knows she will receive everything and be permanently rid of him.

In the situation of CPS determining that her allegations are not indicated, the court will have to grant the father some shared custody time and establish a visitation schedule within the pendente lite order. This will be a setback for the mother, but she did not mourn the injustice for too long. She continued pressing her campaign forward, building her support base through the sharing of her accusations and her consequent hardships. She cries that the system has failed her and her children. She focuses on gathering the support of people from multiple churches. She visits local domestic violence support groups to absorb tactics from other women. She observes how they behave when discussing the horrors that they experienced. She needs to be able to mimic those responses and body language when she makes her future reports. If no one will believe her, then they must believe that she believes her allegations. If the judge will say that the mother believes what she is claiming, no prosecution team in the country will ever prosecute her for making these allegations to law enforcement about a husband sexually abusing his own children. No one will ever take an action that could remotely be seen as punishing a possible victim for coming forward. Too many victims are too frightened to come forward as it is. Their identity is so shattered that they cannot see how anyone could believe them. The mother was not punished for her allegations because of how victims could see it as confirmation that no one would believe, causing them to stay in a disastrous, perhaps lethal, situation.

While the mother regroups after receiving the pendente lite order, she works with her team on developing her next course of action. She is required to allow her children to visit their father, which will provide additional opportunities for her to report additional allegations. If the father has not yet been triggered from the protection from abuse order and the pendente lite order, she will search for more ways to make him act out. Now that there will be exchanges of the children, she can call the police every time she has to see him. She can accuse him of stealing things from the property; claim he has weapons on his person or within his automobile; and of course, the classic claim that he is blocking her path. The mother makes these reports to create chaos maintaining the appearance she truly believes the father will hurt the children. The judge will ensure that law enforcement does not hold the mother accountable for fraud, waste, and abuse of law enforcement resources. She uses this enabling to harass the father into an outburst.

The mother will have wanted her attorney to demand within the pendente lite order that all transportation of her children for exchanges will be carried out by the father, so she has control of the locations, the battlefield. One mother jumped into the father's driver's seat while he was putting his child into their car seat preventing him from being able to leave. She was counting on him touching her elbow or shoulder when he would go to ask her to move out of his automobile so he can leave. All it takes is one finger on her and she can accuse him of assault. The judge will often not consider a statement from a young child if the child's statement helps the man, but if a child can say they saw their father touch the mother's shoulder the judge will ensure the man is charged with assault. When the father returns the children, the mother violently jerks them from his arms and throws them into the house. What father can watch someone throw their young infant child around? The mother can accuse him of threatening her through a look, intended or not is of no consequence. Threats are not always intended but can always be claimed as having been perceived by the victim. That tool is always available to the mother.

Joint Custody and Visitation

What exactly are the different definitions of physical custody?

- Sole physical custody is when the children live with one parent, and the other parent may have some visitation.
- Shared physical custody is when the children live with both parents for significant periods of time.
    ◦ Primary custody, under shared physical custody, is when one parent has the children for a majority of the time. When one parent has primary custody, the other parent has partial custody, less than the majority of the time.

The mother is fighting for sole physical and legal custody with the father completely removed from her children's lives. Her goal has been, is, and will always be to completely alienate her children from their father as quickly as possible so that her coaching will take root deeply and soundly. Her goal is to send him to prison for the rest of his natural life. Unfortunately, she is now having to share custody with the father. She knows that there are sacrifices, but things will be so much better for her and her children when he is finally permanently out of their lives. The mother presses on.

The mother decides to make her next allegation through the child's pediatrician. The pediatrician has not yet been involved, so she will now be introducing a new mandatory reporter into the fold. The pediatrician may have heard minor details about her allegations from the investigators, but not near enough to allow themselves to believe the mother would use her own children in such a manner.

Disbelief and denial are the mother's friend when it comes to the various experts involved. People have a very difficult time imagining a mother could use their children this way. Most people will choose to believe the mother. They will believe that something happened and try to make at least one note revealing the possibility of the child having an indicator present during their exam. However, if the child does not have any of the indicators necessary for a doctor to report sexual abuse, the pediatrician may note that there are no indicators being present and refer the mother to take the children to the Emergency Room for a second opinion. If the pediatrician sees no indicators and does not report the allegation to child protective services, then the mother makes the allegation directly to CPS herself. The mother is enabled to make as many allegations as she desires.

The investigative agencies are going to convene and discuss the mother's current allegations. With the overwhelming absence of any signs of abuse, her allegations will once again be determined as not indicated and no changes made to the visitation schedule set forth by the court. The mother's attorney may explode when they hear of this latest round of accusations the mother has made. Some attorneys do have morals that may get in the mother's way. The mother's attorney may tell her to seek new representation. This is not a bad thing for her. Possibly inconvenient, but not bad. It is not uncommon for a person with these intentions to go through a half dozen attorneys. The judge will applaud the mother for staying on course. The judge will provide the mother with as much time as she needs to find a new attorney, even personally recommending attorneys, with the hopes this additional time will give the man more time to have an outburst before the judge must make a ruling. And, the father, remains financially responsible for paying the mother's attorneys through the divorce!

CHAPTER 4 –
TRY AGAIN

Cease Father's Custody

Thus far the mother's latest allegations have been too small to cease shared custody. The shared custody is destroying the alienation the mother had developed during the PFA. The mother feels like she is losing ground. This enraged her but she used it to motivate herself. CPS has possibly even reported that the mother is coaching the children to try and influence custody. It is time to take it up a notch. The mother will bring an end to shared custody, no matter the method, the cost, nor who she must use, including her children. She will no longer allow her children to speak or see their father again. She must save them herself, but how did she do it?

She calls the police to report sexual abuse of her children by their father. The police come and take her report in person. She does not need to be concerned on whether the children make any accusations. She can have them point to their bottom, or say daddy tickled me, etc. What they do or do not say in this circumstance holds no value as long as the court can use this situation to claim the children were uncomfortable and could not be expected to reveal anything to police officers. She can claim to the police that the father raped her children; that he dances naked in front of them; makes them touch each other, etc. She will immediately be directed by CPS to not permit the father any further access to the children as a new investigation begins.

The investigators of this are going to consist of doctors, CPS,

Child Advocacy Center, District Attorney's office, and of course the police. The investigation may end in a finding of abuse being not indicated. When she is told this, the mother calls a telephone support hotline and again made the claims about the police just not getting it and she insinuates she was close to being suicidal. She made everyone afraid that if they confront her, she might do something bad to herself, or others. The judge will likely be appalled at the audacity that experienced investigators made a judgment call and closed the investigation. The judge will likely try to make the determination of the subject matter experts be meaningless in the trial so that the mother's allegations remain possible rather than rejected.

Unless the father is arrested, he is not going to know anything other than the mother will no longer permit him to have his time with his children. The father will have to have his attorneys file for an emergency contempt of court, due to the mother suddenly blocking his access to his children. A hearing will be scheduled. It will take weeks to months before this hearing can occur. The investigators have told the mother that they concluded their investigation and found that the mother is coaching the children well before the hearing. Regardless, she has her attorney take the police report consisting of the allegation of child rape to the judge at the hearing and claim an investigation is ongoing. The judge is going to agree to keeping the children away from their father until the investigation is complete. It is likely this will be the point in time the judge will appoint a Guardian ad Litem unless the mother has already wisely directed her attorneys to have one appointed. This will be the first time the father and his attorneys become aware of this police report and the father will be required to hire a criminal defense attorney.

If for some reason law enforcement does ever decide to begin looking into the mother concerning her false police reports, she should understand that some states have a one year statute of limitations for this, and some states have a three year statue of limitations. The mother verified which one her state had. The judge will very likely not allow law enforcement to pursue this during the divorce and custody trial, which will make the statute of limitations run out. This would have to be pursued by law enforcement alone, not the father. No officer went against the judge to sign a warrant for this. The mother had nothing to worry about. The judge will assist the mother's attorney in providing her with enough time to surpass statute of limitations in the unlikely event it is even necessary. The judge will normally provide as many continuances as possible that the mother's attorney requests.

Remember creativity creates advantages, and there are many mandatory reporters involved. Therefore, she makes her allegations to different entities each time to rotate who she is making them to. This keeps the mother from overwhelming any one mandatory reporter. The mother is expected to be stressed and concerned, so sympathies will be provided from everyone.

Have Pediatrician Probe Daughter for Chlamydia

At some point during the process the mother decided to make her accusations seem physically plausible. Some of her family or friends are within the medical field, doctors, nurses, counselors, etc. The emergency room, nor the child advocacy center has seen any indication that they need to check the child for a sexually transmitted disease (STD) but the mother knows that sometimes when a child is sexually abused they are checked for an STD. The mother and her medical profession allies discuss this disappointment. It would have appeared better if the mother was not the one to have to direct the procedure, but they need the physical alteration that would be a result of a medical probe. The mother took her child to the pediatrician. She had already made the pediatrician aware of the accusations and she directs the child's pediatrician to probe her child for chlamydia. She specifically directs the doctor to utilize the probe method, rather than a urine sample of swab. The probe inserts the instrument checking the back of the cervix. The judge will ensure no one ever asks too many questions about this procedure. The pediatrician will not testify, they will want nothing to do with any outcomes of committing this atrocity with no indicators justifying it. The probe leaves permanent alterations to a child that can theoretically support future allegations the mother is already preparing for.

CHAPTER 5 – SWARM

Claim Threats to Home Security

Meanwhile the mother is also simultaneously making other chaotic accusations. While she continues trying to make everyone believe the father is raping his own children, she continued trying to convince people she was fearful for her safety from the father. She makes police reports claiming someone is stalking her home and scaring her. She puts on a good show when she makes her report. She uses all tactical advantages at her disposal such as good theatrics, the weaker vessel, a battered woman, all the things she picked up from the other women in the shelter. Someone will advise her that she should install a home security system. She will be expected to use the marital funds to install cameras, gates, locks, etc. These are additional ways to deplete the father's resources. The fewer resources he has, the less counsel he can fund to defend him from the allegations.

When reporting her husband for stalking her, all she needs to do is claim she saw his car setting in her driveway, or somewhere close to her residence. She will not need a shred of evidence. No one will be able to prove that someone wasn't too close to her residence that caused her to fear for her safety. This provides her with additional posturing, more chaos, smoke and mirrors, that the judge can justify inflicting as much pain on the father as possible to get that one negative outburst the court system needs to justify the mother's campaign.

Stalk School Campus inside and out

If the children are back to having visitation with the father, then the mother's work at alienating them from him is in jeopardy. She wanted to remind her children of her presence at every opportunity when they are with the father. The mother randomly shows up at the children's school. She will have already been working with the school counsellors and nurses since the initial accusations were made. Human nature wants to believe the best about people, so the teachers and counsellors will not want to believe the mother is using her children. The father's attorneys will be advising him to not speak to anyone, because nearly all entities involved will be looking for anything he says to use against him, especially if anything appears negative about the mother. Chances are very high that no one at school has any idea that the father has had custody rights reinstated. Most schools allow parents to have an occasional lunch with their child. Due to what the school will believe has happened to the children they will allow the mother more opportunities to visit with her child. They believe they are supporting the children by allowing them extra time with their mother through this traumatic time. Every time she visits with them, she asked them if they feel safe with their dad now; is he hurting you anymore; is daddy nice to you now; etc. She continued to force her narrative into their young impressionable psyches trying to create fear of their father.

Besides lunch opportunities she would take her dog and walk around campus. A mother walking her dog around campus with the accusations she has made appears like a concerned mother wanting to get a spot check on her children. If school staff does approach her, she shares her story, receives their sympathy, and leaves. She will want to coordinate her walk with location and timing of the child's classroom activities such when the child's class is in the hall going to lunch, or on way to and from recess, etc. She needs her children to see her so that they are repetitively reminded about what it is their mother is doing, a fabricated fear of their father.

Due to the nature of her accusations teachers and counsellors eagerly provide her with their personal phone numbers and request that she reach out to them day or night if she needs help. She works these contacts like she does her group of older single women from the churches. The people are going to stick their neck out to help her contact her children and providing her with daily briefings to her on what they have observed concerning her children. It is during these conversations that she has them tell her the inner workings of the campus, and her children's class schedules, when they go out to recess, lunch, PE, etc.

Eavesdropping Device

Whenever her children must visit their father, she can take advantage of this as an optimal means to gather intelligence on him. She needs to find a way to get as much information on him as possible. It is an unfortunate mistake to allow herself to believe she already has everything she needs to know about him. She can never have too much intel. All new information she gathers brings her new options she can twist into additional accusations that she may have not yet considered. One of the best methods to gather intelligence on him is to plant an eavesdropping device, such as an audio recorder, or possibly video recorder. Take advantage of new technology. Many devices are motion or voice activated with hundreds of hours of recording capacity and are small enough to easily be positioned within a child's stuffed animal. Many stuffed animals have a battery pack within them making it quite normal to feel something mechanical within the stuffing which helps mask any notice of her planted eavesdropping device.

There are several good reasons to deliver this stuffed animal with a planted eavesdropping device to the school and request the school be the ones to hand it to her child. The first obvious reason is if the school does not discover the device, then it is the school delivering a cleared toy to her child. She would be depending on her child bringing the stuffed animal back to her at some point to retrieve all intel the device captured. Once the child(ren) return the stuffed animal to her, she would then be able to take the device, download the data, and try to find something else to twist into a new allegation. When her child brings the stuffed animal back to her then she will also have the option to make the accusation to the police that her husband planted the device and have him charged with criminal eavesdropping. She makes sure it records something from her, so that the charge is not just attempted, but that he is charged and convicted of criminal eavesdropping.

Another good reason to take the stuffed animal with a surveillance device in it to the school would be that she is hoping that they do discover the device. Why would she want the school to discover it? So that more people will see her desperation in investigating her predator husband so that she can save her children from him. The judge will lap this up as an act of courage on her part. The judge will excuse her criminal act as being due to the multiple investigations of her husband and the investigators unable to get it right. She must continue playing the part of the unstable, protective mother that wholeheartedly believes her allegations that she continues to fabricate. If the school finds the device and reports this incident to law enforcement, then the device never made it to the husband to record him, therefore the most she can be charged with is attempted criminal eavesdropping. This is a meaningless little class B misdemeanor. It is only a slap on a wrist, but it shows people she is fully engrossed in her belief system and will do whatever it takes to protect her children.

Family Pets

The mother continued to seek new methods to trigger the father into an outburst. Most families have pets. The father was probably the one that took care of these pets, consequently growing close to them. She knows he has not seen them in a year or two, after being kicked out by the PFA. She is the one with the home and the family pets. Poisoning a family pet is something that is incredibly easy to get away with, with no repercussions. The mother would have to be caught on camera forcing a block of rat poison down the throat of the animal before law enforcement would truly investigate the matter. If the father suspects any mistreatment and calls animal control for help to check on his pets, he will be perceived as a spiteful husband going through a nasty divorce. They will send someone to ask the mother about the animals and all she will need to say is the dog ate a poisoned mouse. If there are no photos, or videos, of the mother placing rat poison into the mouth of the pet, the judge will only state that it is impossible to say if the pet dying from rat poison in her care is negligence or intentional. Rat poison is easily accessible at feed stores, hardware stores, even grocery stores. The mother claims that the pet ate a poisoned mouse. It will be months before her husband's attorneys, and then him, will ever learn of the pet's demise. By that time, she already had the pet cremated. No one is going to question this any further at all.

Surely this will get a reaction from the father when he learns that not only is the mother using his children, but she is now killing his beloved pets with rat poison. She only needs to continue finding ways to trigger an outburst from him. She never stopped seeking a reaction to use against him. She is saturating the battlefield. She created chaos in every area she could. Creativity creates advantages. She has been using her own children's innocence, killing a pet will be easier than it sounds, and the end justifies the means.

Part Time Work

One of the mother's claims is the father would not allow her to follow her dreams. So now that she has gotten the home, the money, and him out of her life, her support group is taking it upon themselves to create job opportunities for her. They are getting her interviews, or scheduling appointments with university admissions counsellors. They are advising her to prove to others that she can work and provide a decent life on her own for herself and her child(ren.) Unfortunately, she will need to entertain them to a point so that her stories remain plausible. She will only have to try and keep a job, or go to classes, for a couple weeks before she can drop out and return to her full-time pursuit of destroying the father. She can blame her lack of commitment on the extreme fear and stress she is under, as she is worried about her children's safety. They will all believe she tried and will understand that she is not able to move forward yet because of the father. A judge will applaud her attempt to work.

The court will typically order in the final divorce that the husband provide her spousal support for a set time to maintain her expected lifestyle. The mother knows that had she kept a job then he would have to pay less. Any amount he is not giving to her he is able to send to his defense attorneys. The mother is always looking for ways to drain his resources, even if it is not going to her. Whatever dime he can hold onto, he is able to invest that into defense to climb out from under the allegations she placed upon his shoulders.

The mother's work schedule could impact child custody in the event the father has survived her allegations and has received some version of shared custody. If she holds a job before the custody case is decided, and the father has the more flexible work schedule, then he could be given more parenting time with the children in the final custody schedule. If she holds a job that requires her to relocate, this could also impact custody. Due to the high conflict case, it is wise to consider slowly seeking employment following the final divorce order, and possibly begin a new job right before the custody trial. The mother balances the timing with the lessons she learns from her support group of women that have been through the system. Her goal is to bleed the man dry for as long as she can, but she may also need to present at custody trial an appearance of being capable of providing for her children financially.

Deposition

Before the trial, within the discovery period, there will be an event called the deposition. A deposition is conducted on the plaintiff and the defendant to provide the attorneys with an opportunity to get information on the case. Depositions are usually held at the questioning attorney's office. For example, the mother's attorney will depose the father at his or her law firm, and then his attorney will depose the mother at his or her law firm. Depositions are under oath and recorded by a court reporter. The major areas of question are finances; recreational activities; alcohol and drug use; specifics on the accusations; and medical issues such as mental health, etc. The participants of the depositions are the attorneys, the mother, the father, and the court reporter. If the mother was born in a different country or grew up in a home that speaks a different language, she should request a translator. It will not matter if she grew up speaking English, she will be permitted to have a translator present at all events. This provides her opportunity after each question at deposition, and trial, to consider her response as she requests the translator to repeat a question to her in the foreign language.

The mother's attorney will provide her beforehand with the standard rules of engagement for the deposition: do not respond until she has properly considered her response and waited for her attorney to object when needed; only provide the answer to the question; ask for clarification whenever she does not understand the question; and she can say she does not know, or she does not recall.

The father's attorney may reveal much within the mother's deposition. This annoyed the mother, but it is only a formality. A box to check. She can respond to interrogatories and discovery in incomplete answers and wait until the evening before or morning of the deposition to submit them. A judge will ensure she is provided top cover as long as she has responded with something. The mother claims to be confused, but still responded with something and in the eyes of the judge she has made a good faith effort to respond. It is very common for the woman to be able to repeatedly perjure herself without any sort of repercussions. The mother can literally laugh in the face of the opposing attorney trying to question her. Most attorneys know the judge will hold it against them if they press the woman too hard, so she enjoys the spotlight laughing, crying, not recalling as many things as she wishes, and asking for breaks to compose herself. Alternatively, her attorney will be expected to be extremely aggressive towards the father. Her attorney will look for any information they can use against her husband at trial. The mother's attorney make him commit to statements under oath. The mother's attorney tries to twist every response because he will be held accountable for any perjury he may commit.

The mother had her attorney schedule both the mother and father's deposition to be on two consecutive days. The mother had her attorneys schedule her deposition to be conducted on day one. The father will have scheduled his days off with his boss weeks in advance. The day the mother's deposition arrives, everyone comes together for the deposition, and as it begins the mother created a reason, she is unable to proceed. She claimed an illness, something particularly womanly that no one will question. The father's attorney will request to proceed with the father's deposition. The mother has her attorney claim to not be prepared to proceed with the father's deposition. This will cancel the entire first day of the deposition. The father will have to pay for everyone's time, including the court reporter that was there to transcribe the entire deposition. The mother always seeking ways to make the father sink further into debt. She is always looking for something to cause the father to react negatively. Everyone is looking for any reason to believe he is the abusive monster she claims him to be. She just needs him to have one outburst. She believes she will get one eventually. The mother stays on target.

Attorneys Withdrawing

It is acceptable and expected for someone with a strong agenda to go through a half dozen attorneys or more. The judge will not find any suspicion on a mother going through multiple attorneys. Whenever an attorney of the mother's withdraws from her case she does not fret, she adaptively moved on to the next one that she had kept her interviewing notes for. She continues to micromanage each one, and watches what they do because it is often strategically a good idea for her to consider representing herself pro se once she has found comfort in the process. When the mother represents herself, the judge is able to compassionately grant the mother more leeway. A judge will engage even to the point of directly rephrasing the pro se mother's trial questions of the father to steer them within the narrative being sought. If the father does not have good counsel, then the mother's victory is certain.

Even though the mother does not face accountability for her actions in pursuing her agenda, there could be times that one of her attorney's misconducts while serving her are unable to be overlooked. At these times the state bar association may require the mother's attorney to withdraw from the case. The mother's attorney may be required to state that if they continue to represent her it would make continued representation of her in this matter a violation of the mother's state's rules of professional conduct. States have rules of misconduct for attorneys to abide by. They all share some very common language within Rule 8.4 for Misconduct. This rule defines professional misconduct that if a lawyer commits, then they must withdraw from the case. The attorney must also withdraw if they know they are about to commit a misconduct. This is not a may withdraw situation, it is a shall withdraw requirement set forth within governing laws. If an attorney violates, or attempt to violate, the rules of their state's professional conduct, or knowingly helps another to do so, or even if they violate through the acts of another person then they must submit a motion to the court to withdraw with reason as counsel for their client. Obviously if an attorney commits a criminal act that reflects adversely on the lawyer's honesty, trustworthiness, or fitness as a lawyer in other respects then he or she must file a motion to withdraw as the mother's counsel. If the mother's attorney gets caught engaging in fraud, deceit, or misrepresentation they must withdraw. If the mother's attorney gets caught engaging in conduct that is prejudicial to the administration of justice, then they must withdraw. If the mother's attorney gets caught making any attempt at unethically swaying governmental opinion involving the case, then they must exit as the mother's representation. If the attorney knowingly assists a judge commit a violation of law; or knowingly fails to comply with a final court order entered in a proceeding in which the lawyer is a party; or threatens to seek criminal charges only to obtain an advantage in a civil matter, then the mother's attorney must withdraw as her legal counsel.

It is critical that the mother find an attorney that she can micromanage through the ins and outs of the system together and not get caught circumventing ethical processes throughout her case. If the mother has an attorney that is required to withdraw, this is at most inconvenient. The court system will applaud the attorney and the mother for their bravery against the superior man, and the court will likely go as far as to recommend to her a new attorney that will progress the narrative, one that conveniently has an axe to grind with the father's attorney. There are dozens of available attorneys waiting for a client like the mother that will do anything to win. They consider these cases like sports games, counting wins versus losses. Good attorneys want to win. The mother should ask her support group, including the judge, for any recommendations of retired highly successful attorneys. The mother needs to find an attorney that is willing to destroy a man at any cost.

Status Hearing(s) Before Divorce Order

There may be status hearings before the divorce trial. Status hearings are for the judge to touch base with the mother and father's attorneys while both parties are present. If there is a guardian ad litem, GAL, then they will be present as well. The mother did not have representation for this hearing, and she chose to dramatically throw herself at the mercy of the court. The mother appeared disheveled and confused and tells the judge that she no longer wants the divorce. This will throw everyone in the courtroom off balance. Creativity creates advantage. The mother creates controlled chaos whenever possible. The father's attorney and GAL arrived at this hearing prepared for what they were going to present and now upon hearing the mother no longer wanting to pursue divorce will forget what that was. The judge will ask the father if he wants to consider reconciliation.

The mother knows he will respond that he will not consider any marital reconciliation at this point, so there is no risk to the mother for making these confusing statements. The mother's goal is to create opportunities through chaos. Her statement increases the judge's sympathy for the mother. Now the father is the one demanding the divorce to this distraught mother who is obviously at her wits end, and without any representation against the superior man.

Once everyone has heard the mother say she no longer want the divorce, she will need to immediately make another allegation about her husband such as he is interfering with her work in some way, stalking her, harassing her, etc. She says he discovered where she works at from the deposition. She says she sees him driving by her work multiple times, which terrifies her and interferes with her productivity at the job. The new accusation's truth cannot be verified, but the mother is providing the judge with something to aggressively question the husband about right there under observation within the hearing. It is all smoke and mirrors, but the judge is not going to look behind the curtain to see who the puppet master really is. The judge will strictly order the husband that if the judge learns that he is interfering with her ability to make money then he will be going to jail. The mother enjoys watching the father be threatened with jail time, while she is comforted and enabled.

She discusses at the hearing her financial woes. Even though her husband is following the status quo order of the pendente lite order funding her lifestyle, she says she does not have any money. This is once again providing the judge with something to threaten the father with jail time. As the alleged battered woman, the mother is enabled and encouraged to claim anything she wants. When she may face any questions, she does not provide clear responses. She provided twisted, confusing, responses. She plays the part of the weaker vessel, confused, just doing the best she can, she may have been mistaken about this or that, etc. The mother only needs to show an attempt at making responses to questions. The judge wants to help this sad mother.

If she chose to plant any eavesdropping devices in toys to spy on the father, and it was discovered, she chose to be the one to bring this out in the open at the hearing. She tells the judge how she had to do something to investigate the father since the investigators are incapable of performing their jobs. She accuses each agency, law enforcement, CPS, the GAL, counsellors, etc. of not being able to properly execute their jobs. She says they are liars. She tells the judge she saw no other choice but to do something. The judge will have compassion and sympathy for her. The judge will likely recommend attorneys by name to her in a status hearing telling her they will be pro bono for her, yet once the mother hires one the judge will order the father pay the new mother's new pro bono attorney a retainer.

Divorce Trial

At the trial for the divorce the mother's attorney will focus on assassinating the character of the father to try and get a negative outburst from him in front of the judge. Her attorney will also need to diligently put on record that the mother wholeheartedly believes that the father is and has sexually abused his children. Her husband needs to be placed on the stand from the very beginning of the trial as a hostile witness. This will be the first true impression the judge is getting of the father. Her attorney needs to twist and antagonize the father. The judge will permit her attorney to harass the father and will prevent his attorney from making the mother uncomfortable when she is on the stand. It is the mother's responsibility to either have an attorney that is on the same page with her on destroying a good man or having an attorney she can micromanage and direct what questions they need to ask the father. This will ensure the dozens of accusations made over the past year or two are slung against the wall to try and provide one the judge can make seem plausible for the record.

Both parties' attorneys will have requested information before the trial such as, but not limited to:
- monthly bank statements,

- monthly credit card statements,
- income tax returns,
- bills of sale,
- mortgage documents,
- retirement accounts, IRAs, 401(k)s,
- household bills and proofs of payments.

The man is not permitted to ignore these requests, and any difficulty he and his attorney have in submitting them to the mother's attorney in advance of the trial will be seen and taken by the judge as dishonesty. However, the weaker vessel is permitted by the judge to respond to the request with one or two of the requested documents the business day before the trial and encouraged to submit surprise submittals as exhibits during the trial, and immediate questioning of the blindsided husband. If the woman submits a few of the requests the judge will dictate that the mother and her attorney have acted in a good faith effort.

The judge will typically not require the mother to verify things she claims such as, but not limited to:
- minimizing and hiding income or assets,
- minimizing how much the father contributed to household finances,
- misleading how joint finances were spent,
- accusing the father of stealing money from her and any joint business ventures,
- accusing the father of having affairs, use of drugs and alcohol, abuse, etc.

The mother remembered to use terms such as:
- to the best of my knowledge,
- I do not recall,
- as I recall,
- I will have to get back with you on that
- I have no way of knowing that because he took that with him

The judge will be satisfied with the mother responding in such manner. The judge will require the man to provide absolute and immediate responses to all questions from the mother's attorney and will personally question the father if it seems her attorney is forgetting to ask something. The judge will drive the car to keep it on the narrative that the judge is pursuing for the record. If the husband thinks too long before responding to any question the judge will accuse him of being dishonest or misleading. The judge will accuse him of taking time to construct dishonest responses. The mother's attorney began by accusing him of the worst things a father can do to his children. The father is rattled. Nerves that he worked on overcoming for months trying to mentally prepare for this week are betraying him. The mother has her attorney press harder. In his rattled state, he will space out and this will create pauses before he responds. This provides the judge ample opportunities to direct the husband to stop taking so long to respond making it appear for the record he is calculating his responses before making them. The mother's attorney and the judge are working in tandem swatting the father back and forth to maintain the narrative they need for the record to be able to give the mother sole custody.

The mother has isolated the father from his friends and family that she could during the marriage and has caused countless more to abandon him following her accusations over the past couple years. The fruits of her labors have had the father isolated for years. She has caused him to burn through all of his resources, as well as that of the few allies that stuck with him through hell to survive her allegations just so that he could be able to help his children. If he has lasted this long without an outburst that the judge could use against him, then his patience is stretched so thin that he is prime for an outburst or a mental break down. At the very least while he is hearing these accusations for the first time come out of the lips he once kissed, as well as the barrage from the mother's attorney and the judge, he may sob. If the father so much as silently cries and the judge observes a tear upon his cheek, the judge will stop the trial and ask what the husband is sobbing for. The judge will likely take the opportunity to ask if the husband is sobbing, due to a guilty conscience.

When the mother is under oath, on the record, she decided to lie about some of the accusations she has made. Even if her accusations are documented by the witnesses that she made these accusations to, doctors, CPS, counsellors, the guardian ad litem, she needs to lie about making each one that did not pan out. The judge will not allow her to be pressed on anything she could perjure herself on. The mother never lets go of claiming her child made an accusation to her at the beginning. She can claim that her child made additional accusations to her over the years, and is just too scared, embarrassed, or doesn't want to hurt their daddy, etc. Even a successfully passed polygraph by the father will not stop the judge from helping the mother claim her child has or is making these allegations only to her and no one else. Her attorney and the judge will aggressively attack the professionalism and credibility of all expert witnesses, even court appointed experts, that are not supporting her allegations. She will want to direct her attorney to know the backgrounds of the expert witnesses, their credentials; publications; active professional memberships and licenses, what they got their education in; where they got their education; how long they have worked in this area; where do they work now, etc. Her attorney needs to be prepared to attack every person that the father's attorney has subpoenaed to trial.

One of the subject matter experts, which will likely have been appointed by name by the judge, is a psychiatrist that performed the psychological evaluations on the mother and father. If she happened to have been diagnosed with anything, her attorney will need to have already spun a defense that the judge can use to break holes in. Every expert that is appointed by the judge knows that the judge sends them clients, and a portion of their future bottom line is based upon how well the judge likes them. Consequently, they will have been educated on what the narrative is the judge is pursuing, and they will either diagnose her with nothing or something very minor that very lightly touches upon what it is she should be treated for. With a minimal diagnosis her attorney and judge will be able to tag team the psychiatrist on a diagnosis, no matter how experienced they may be, it remains one person's opinion based on tests that are difficult for a mother in her condition to focus and adequately take. This will poke plausible holes of the diagnosis being based on inadequate information, for the record. The mother does not worry about anything she may be diagnosed with in a court appointed psychological evaluation.

As with any court order, many directives within it are in reality optional for the mother. The final decree will have more weight than the orders issued during the divorce, but there will be several insignificant items listed within it. If the judge orders the father to pay the mother a certain amount and gives the mother a date to be out based on when he transfers that amount to her, then she must adhere to the big items of taking the money, but she can drag her feet on when it is she decides to vacate the home. It is possibly he has not been in his home for years at this point since she had him kicked out by law enforcement based on her accusations. If she waits a week or two to leave the house he may explode or have to spend additional resources to call for an emergency hearing. Law enforcement will not get involved with a civil matter, based on a decree. They will not remove a mother from the home until there is an order issued by the judge directing the police to remove her. She would learn if the judge signs such an order and she would leave before the police execute that order. She responded she was confused about the date and was trying to fulfill the requirements of the decree. The judge will assign new requirements based on her good faith efforts. She will not face any accountability for it, but she could get an outburst from the father that she could use for the custody trial. If she is to hand over any personal items, she likely already threw it in the garbage or sold it. Again, the father will have to burn through additional resources to call for a hearing about it and then she can just claim she thought she had it, but he had already taken it with him. Very little, if anything is verified. It is word against word and the mother wins. She would have to sell the house after the divorce, or something extremely drastic for the judge to have to hold the mother in contempt. The mother already knew that she could get away with murdering a family pet, so she continued to do everything she could to press the father. The mother must be brave against the superior man.

It is critical that she never allows herself to be intimidated by a divorce trial. The judge will ensure it is the mothers to lose. Most information she will find on what to expect from a divorce are written according to the rule of law, with the idea that a person is innocent until proven guilty beyond a reasonable doubt. The books and other materials are written without incorporating the impact the bias the judicial system has for the woman versus the man. This is because the judge takes an oath that includes neutrality. The mother can learn definitions, processes, roles and responsibilities, but she takes her actual advice from the support group she has built of women that have been through, and successfully used the system. Some of them have experience in abusing the tipped balance of the system to bankrupt and destroy their ex's.

Divorce Order

After the divorce trial both parties will receive the final divorce decree. It has likely been nearly two years now since the father was kicked out of the house by law enforcement due to the mother's PFA based on her allegations of sexual abuse of his children. The mother needs to continue pursuing negative reactions from the father, never letting up, that she can use in the upcoming custody trial. She likely still has some family pets he was close to and has not seen in two years. Now is an optimal time to poison another family pet. The ends justify the means. Surely if she kills another one of the family pets, she can get a reaction from him. So, she made another one disappear and waited as long as she could to let anyone know that the pet was gone. She says this one ran out rather than saying it ate a poisoned mouse. She says she looked everywhere and talked to neighbors in her search.

The judge will not even consider the witness of these neighbors saying she never once spoke to them about a missing pet.

If the decree awards any items to the father, the court will overlook if the mother mysteriously lost possession of them before the transfer of said assets back to him. The court does not care what the mother gives back to the father. To the court it is all out of sight and out of mind. The mother is free to take this opportunity to cause the father further pain. The decree may require her to give him items back such as: tools, machines, cattle, websites, something that he had used to make additional money before he was kicked out. She must deplete all his resources and his ability to acquire new resources he could use to defend himself with. She damages his reputation everywhere she can and make what assets she can disappear. If he has his attorneys approach the court that she has not fulfilled her responsibilities set forth in the decree, all she will need to do is have her attorney respond she is looking for something, or he took it with him when he was kicked out, etc. This allows the judge to say she is trying to fulfill her part of the order in good faith. No one pressed the mother any further than that. Meanwhile she has caused the father to burn through more resources for nothing. The less he has the lower his odds of digging himself out from under future allegations.

Custody Hearing(s)

When the day of the custody trial begins, the mother may find that the court appointed counsellors and the guardian ad litem have seen through her allegations and are not too fond of how she is using her children for her agenda. Some people's morals will overcome their loyalty to the judge's narrative, to a point. They may report to the judge in chambers, or even testify, that the mother is not a safe parent for the children. This is of no concern. The judge will more than likely threaten to replace them. The judge controls what they want entered onto the record, even preventing facts that stain the desired narrative, and can absolutely shut the trial down to schedule a new one. The judge knows the counselors have a portfolio built upon a bottom line met by the cases the judge directs to them. The court will direct the cast to fulfill the narrative of the children needing to be with the mother no matter how abusive the mother is, or the judge will threaten to replace them. If the threats to the experts' bottom line brings them back into submission, the judge will likely reschedule the hearing for about twelve months out to provide the experts time to reevaluate the information they came with today, and hopefully enough time for new allegations to lead the father into a negative outburst.

Upon learning that yet another hearing has been set and the mother did not receive sole custody, it is critical that the mother take her attorney and the guardian ad litem outside the courtroom and execute a complete meltdown screaming at them. While the mother screams at them she will let them know how inept everyone is and they are allowing the father to get away with sexually abusing his children. The mother will have already instructed her friends to come and join in on this attack of the GAL. The mother knows the court's goal of the mother having the children at all cost. The mother knows the GAL is not going to go against the judge's narrative. The judge is not going to allow any law enforcement to contain or reprimand the distraught mother. The mother is creating a dramatic performance to gain more sympathy as the concerned weaker vessel. This provides the mother with more time to continue coaching her children and make more allegations! More allegations mean the mother has more opportunities to have the father thrown in jail! The judge will directly advise the mother that the court needs the mother to bring the court evidence. The mother is being enabled. If at first the mother does not succeed, the court will provide her with ample opportunities to keep trying.

Physical Abuse

The mother is fully aware that most people are unable to fathom a mother could hurt her own children, and she also knows that the judicial system views the woman as the weaker vessel that must have as much custody as possible. It is the mother's case to lose. Many people believe a person would have their children taken away from them if they as so much as spanked their child. Many people believe corporal punishment to be illegal. This is not the case. CPS seems to require a child's bone be violently broken on camera before children could be considered to be taken away from their mother. A mother is permitted to hit her children, if she does not cross a line no one seems to have clearly defined. It is open to judgement, and by the time any mother crosses that line they are provided get well treatment plans and can easily back off from the violence with no repercussions. It appears the most accountability a mother would receive is to attend a class for breaking a child's bones and all is forgiven. The mother is oftentimes encouraged to use corporal punishment if she is claiming they are acting poorly to her because of parental alienation the father is doing to them.

There are so many examples of women hitting their children with switches, spoons, flip flops, etc. and facing no consequences. The mother has left welts and bruises that last weeks on the child, and the child reports it by themselves to doctors and the judge does not say a single word to the mother about it, and further not permit the father's attorneys and the father to elaborate upon it in the trial. The mother is enabled to utilize fear in her parental alienation and attempts to force allegations.

While the mother is coaching the children she is consistently referring to her allegations as the "real truth." This creates a very beneficial outcome for the mother. The mother knows that investigators will speak to the children during the investigations. As the children respond to the questions and participate in these discussions, they are going to share their experiences, and repeat some things the mother tells them. If the child is not cooperating with the mother's coaching, if they share what it is their mother is trying to make them repeat as their experiences to the investigators, they are going to repeat what the mother is telling them. As they repeat their mother, the child is going to refer to the allegations as the "real truth." These are little nuggets that create enough plausibility to protect the mother. An example is a child is talking to a counselor and says mommy was hitting me for not telling the "real truth." The mother has programmed the child to call the allegations the "real truth." If the child repeats what the mother calls the allegations even once, then within the child interviews or sessions the mother's allegations receive some possibility. Only the mother will know how much coaching the child can handle, but she will have no trouble manipulating them. The mother will never be held accountable. The ends justify the means in crafting his fall to get it all.

Finding a New Doctor

After approximately six months to a year into the divorce process the mother will find that the pediatrician is transitioning into more of a listening role. The mother will pick up on this change of energy. Where once the pediatrician was leading and guiding the mother with questions about her child, they are now quietly taking notes while the mother found herself stumbling with her story. All the creativity is on the mother's shoulders now. This does not concern the mother; she only needs to prepare for this and have her lines memorized so that she is not caught off guard and does stumble around while she is no longer being led with questions to respond to.

What may have occurred is the investigators and GAL have been having discussions with the pediatrician. The pediatrician will learn that the father has not been incarcerated, possibly even has non-supervised visitation. This either means the father is innocent, or the investigators have still not yet acquired enough facts to satisfy the district attorney. Both of those options mean the pediatrician must make sure their files are done properly because they will be looked at. Many pediatricians will begin to feel like they are being used and they will distance themselves from the mother and her allegations.

How is this not bad for the mother? Because the mother is completely aware that the judge has tasked the mother with creating facts that can be used to ensure she gets sole custody. The

GAL is the arm of the judge to guide the narrative as much as the GAL is willing to. Rather than the GAL going against the judge, the mother notices some entities are being guided to distance themselves from the mother while they ensure the law is unable to hold the mother accountable. At times they are preventing some of the mother's excessive accusations from being reported to CPS. When these things begin to happen, after approximately six months to a year into the divorce process, the mother began doctor shopping.

Doctor shopping is self-explanatory. The mother consults her inner circle of women that have been through the system, and possibly personally know pediatricians they can talk to on her behalf. She also pursued small pediatric clinics that are completely unaware of her history. They are all mandatory reporters, and the mother has charismatically perfected her story. Before the mother visits the next doctor, she threatens her child into agreeing to say that the father did such and such. The mother will believe the child is ready, either through fear, promised reward, or whatever manipulation tailored to encourage and motivate the child. When they get to the doctor, she uses her charisma and theatrics to tell the doctor privately about all the many times the supposed sexual abuses have occurred to the child and by the father in the past and say that there are currently ongoing investigations. The mother tells everyone that will listen through the process that the father is being investigated for sexual abuse of his child. Again, she received no accountability for these accusations. She cries to the doctor how no one has been able to help protect her children. She asks them for their help.

After the mother has her time with the doctor, the doctor will see the patient, the child. The mother ensures she is in the room with her child while the doctor examines the child. The mother makes sure the child sees her to try and keep the child afraid to not repeat what has been rehearsed. Some doctors will request that the mother leave the room before carrying out an ethical examination of the child. The mother was so nervous wondering if her child properly executed her commands. However, the mother should not be concerned. She will know soon enough on whether the child repeated the mother's allegation or said that the mother was trying to make her say something. Either way the judge is not going to care if the child corroborates the accusation or not. This new doctor knows the mother is a concerned parent and upon her allegations alone should report the situation to CPS for investigation. The judge needs something like this to support the narrative that the children must be with their mother. The mother remained on course.

The mother did not inform the father about these doctor visits. The father's attorney, the father, nor even the GAL will expect other doctors becoming involved until weeks to months later as the investigations are executed. Not only could they assist in getting the mother permanent sole custody, but they could in fact allow the judge to give her custody through the custody proceedings with the father having no contact or supervised visits. Regardless of what comes of these visits to random uninvolved pediatricians, she can usually expect that only these doctors' reports will successfully be subpoenaed. The doctors do not want to testify. So, she can expect the doctors to put as little as possible within their reports, allowing her attorney room to support the judge's narrative.

Emotional Abuse

This is a long and intense process. Several years are not unusual for a contested divorce and conflicts expound with custody involved. Through this process the children will get older. They are more aware than anyone what abuses the mother has inflicted upon them. They will grow wearisome with the mother's constant coaching and slowly begin to experiment at defying her demands. They will begin to rebel against her directives. They will want to live with their father, and at times she will scream at them to just go live with their father, possibly even kicking them out of the house. They are sick of her lies. They cannot understand the things she put them through. They feel safe at their father's house. They have peace there. The mother is not capable of properly loving her children, but she cannot lose the control, so she uses a village to raise her children.

The mother and her closest allies continued to try and coach the children against their father. Some children will not budge from the truth. She will be so angry with them for this. They are her property that are supposed to do her bidding. The mother and her friends have showered them with gifts. But they will still not give in. So, she waits until nightfall and tells the children that she is going to take them to a certain mandatory reporter such as a new pediatrician, or a school counsellor, etc., and there they are to report her latest allegation. When they do not give in, she screams at them to stop protecting their father and tell them to leave the house right now, at night, and go live with their father. She does not allow them access to a phone. She walks them out of the house and leaves them outside with nowhere to go and no way of contacting anyone. The mother does not pursue them. She does not lock the door. She knows they will not go far and return inside eventually. She is always finding ways to break their spirit down so she can rebuild them into what it is she needs them to be to best serve her. She repeated this as necessary to break the child's security and never know what their mother will do. She is making sure they learn that they are there to satisfy her needs and that when they are with her, no one can make the mother stop. Their father will not learn of this for weeks and cannot help them. If CPS ever asks her about it, she just claims that she did put them out of the house but that she remained in the doorway never losing sight of them. To CPS this is an acceptable form of discipline for the mother to give her children.

Discipline by Others

While the judge and CPS enables the mother to put bruises upon her children, it would still not be wise to press it too far or too often. Remember the line is gray where exactly it lies on how much a mother is permitted to abuse her children. It is completely left to the discretion of the CPS investigator, if it is ever even looked at since it is an act committed by the mother. If she does begin to cross a line for the investigator then the judge and GAL will ensure that the investigator addresses it verbally with her, providing her with the time to back off without any repercussions, off the record. Therefore, the mother encourages her posse of supporters, especially the middle aged to elderly women, to use corporal punishment on her children. The older women receive the same leeway from CPS that mother does so they will oftentimes get away with abusing children just like she has. This is advantageous to the mother's goals by sending her message to her children even when she is not around. And provides her time between her corporal coachings.

Throughout this journey she will have gathered a multitude of supporters without much effort. Through the churches and shelters the mother attends she will have people that wholeheartedly carries her banner. There will be some that are aware of her agenda, and others that believe the children are brainwashed and protecting a guilty father. Several of these people will believe in doing whatever it takes to protect the children, even after hearing with their own ears that multiple investigators have determined that she is coaching the children to sway custody, as well as even learning the father has successfully passed a polygraph upon the matter.

While most of these supporters will be middle-aged to elderly, do not discount the value of a naive young man. It is so very easy for a woman to wrap a young man around her finger. Young men full of hormones rather than sense will carry out hostile acts for a woman leading them on. The next young man to hurt another man due to a woman's story will not be the first nor last to do such. Imagine the possibilities the mother could influence a young man to do to the father based on her perfected story that he is sexually abusing his children. These young men are disposable trinkets that can do sloppy tasks for the mother, and quickly be dismissed.

Mediation

A couple months before the custody trial, the mother directs her attorney to schedule a mediation with the father and his attorneys. She will not have any intention of cooperating for a joint custody scenario. When the mediation begins, she will tell the mediator that she is there to get sole custody and any additional assets from the father that she still wants. She will want to ask for whatever holds any monetary value. She develops a list beforehand and take it with her. The assets were already divided in the divorce decree the previous year, so this will begin the mediation by shocking the ex-husband, his attorney as well as the mediator that has hopes of reaching some version of a meaningful mediation.

The father will respond that he is wanting to offer joint custody. When this happens just return that along with her having sole custody, she will offer him some of the money that she took from him for him to walk away selling his children to her. If there is something that is monetary that has not reached her yet, such as retirement account, etc. that is not money out of her current account, but that is coming to her. To reach this point she will have wanted her and her attorney to have held conversations if possible to draw out the amount of time spent incurring legal fees. Do not even wait for a response from the father after offering this money for his children and just leave. She has caused the father to spend thousands of more dollars for his attorney fees for a mediation she never intended to cooperate in. Again, always seek opportunities to make the father have an outburst. Always seek ways in which to drain his limited resources. A man with no resources is unable to defend himself from allegations. The woman has an unlimited amount of support in all professions, whereas the man has practically zero, when it comes to her alleging sexual abuses.

Custody Trial

The custody trial is only a formality within the American judicial system since sole custody is the mothers to lose. The judge has long decided before the trial began that she would receive sole custody and her wrong doings will be covered up as much as possible. The burden of proof lies heavily upon the father's shoulders. No matter the facts. No matter the testimony of subject matters experts, even those court appointed. The judge will revive her allegations, giving them credence, and constantly creating plausibility for the record to bolster the judge's narrative. However, the judge will still need to put on the appearance of considering the different versions of custody.

- Sole physical custody is when the children live with one parent, and the other parent may have some visitation.
- Shared physical custody is when the children live with both parents for significant periods of time.
  - Primary custody, falling under shared physical custody, is when one parent has the children for a majority of the time. When one parent has primary custody, the other parent has partial custody, less than the majority of the time.

The assets of the marriage will have been divvied out the year before within the divorce decree therefore at this point she is having to pay for her own attorney fees. For appearances of the struggling pitiful woman and to have more time to concentrate her coaching and parental alienation she has not held a job. It is not a bad idea for her to represent herself pro se for the custody trial. It is customary for a judge to allow more freedom within the trial for a pro se. She will be allowed to lead in her questioning. Most, if not all the father's attorney's objections will be overruled. The judge will personally rephrase many of her questions to maintain the desired narrative. And as her own attorney she will have access to investigations of the minor children privy only to the judge and attorneys. This will provide her with more information that the ex-husband is not even aware of and being wholeheartedly engaged in her own plot she will be able to twist all available information that is on record to her desire.

She will see records concerning the children's counsellors, guardian ad litem, conflict counsellor, CPS, psychiatrist, etc. and be aware of which one has seen through her allegations. The records will give her a good idea on which one's conscious may cause them to testify strongly against her. She can always hire a good attorney that will do this for her, but that attorney likely has dozens of other cases floating through their mind. This is the mother's circus, and only she and the children know what all she has done to them. Being her own attorney at this point, and after watching and learning from attorneys over the past couple years through the divorce trial, can greatly assist her campaign.

By representing herself, she will be the one questioning the father. The man that has lost everything because of the mother's allegations. The trauma she has inflicted upon him may cloud his judgement allowing her to lead him in questions to support her narrative. Between her and the judge's help, his trauma may taint his responses with ire that she and the judge can paint as being hostile, or his long pauses of confusion as being less than forthcoming. The judge will try to bait him to contempt to hold him in contempt giving him several weekends of jailtime. She will want to try bringing out any negativity from him that she can to help to help in this baiting him.

With all she has learned these past couple years, representing herself pro se will just be another game for her to enjoy. With her acting skills, weaker vessel when being questioned by his attorney, to a manipulative narcissist when questioning the father, this will be fun and quite beneficial for her. She would have to murder the children to lose custody of them. She can literally be turning tricks on the weekends, have white powder on her upper lip, bruise her children, have them probed for an STD to support her allegations, and she will still get at a minimum joint custody. There is not much risk in representing oneself in this point of the process.

The Father's Financials

After the conclusion of the divorce and the custody court dates, she can begin making use of the personally identifiable information she still has to harass the father's financials. When she had him kicked out of the house via the Protection from Abuse order he very likely left behind his passport, his birth certificate, his computer, his tablet, medications, and everything he was not wearing at the time, or possibly allowed to put into one bag. He likely had his personal computer and tablet save his passwords so that every app or website would automatically log in from his home devices. If she has not already changed his passwords so she can have control. Log in to all the various accounts and make revisions that will create chaos. The trials are over, and he will have to drain additional resources to go back to court for the judge to only tell the ex-husband to address each account to regrant him access with no proof she is the one to have created the chaos. Holding all this information provides her with a means of harassing him when it comes to his finances. The primary reason she married this man was due to his financial acumen. He is fiscally responsible and any harassment of his financials she can deliver should create a negative outburst due to the pressure his enormous debts are weighing on him that placed him in.

The mother has the father's social security number, his email address, his name, birthdate, phone number, his address, etc. She probably has photos of his driver's license. She is aware if he files his taxes online. She knows which online applications he uses to send and receive money. She needs to continue to wear him down for an outburst even after these initial trials. Some women choose to create profiles of their ex-husband on dating websites, especially same sex dating sites. Some women also do this for any allies the ex-husband has. Creativity creates opportunities and advantages.

Her accusations are not complete, and quite possibly never will be. She must ensure he does not get his feet back under him. Visit sites such as PayPal, Amazon, eBay, Citi Card, CashApp, TurboTax, H&R Block, etc. and attempt to login with his email addresses and phone numbers that she already knows. She can guess at passwords she does not have. When the attempted passwords do not log in for her, then click on the option that she has forgotten her password. If he activated the two-step verification and it prevents her from going further, this will send him a text notifying him of his passcode to proceed with logging in to an account he is not logging into. Know that as he receives these messages it is harassing him which is a success. If she does by chance guess the correct password then login and have fun moving funds, cancelling orders, changing passwords and phone numbers, etc. Any person would be troubled if his financials are being hacked or attempted to be hacked into, especially someone fiscally responsible like the father that she put deep into debt through her multiple allegations. Keeping him stressed is the equivalent of keeping him on the ropes. As soon as she executes her next allegation it could be an uppercut sending him once and for all to the mat. She can succeed at completely removing him from the picture.

Custody Order

Her allegations have likely provided everything she needed to receive sole custody, but she could end up with joint legal and joint physical custody. At this point the case could be 3 or more years in the making already. Everyone is tired of it, and the order will reflect that. Usually concise and to the point. The decree will detail custody and visitation rules and schedules. The decree will also list which parent has primary authority and responsibility of the following activities: academic; religious; civic; cultural; athletic; and medical/dental. There may be some restrictions on travelling across state lines and possibly international travel limitations as well. Finally, the one most important to the mother is the child support. The amount of child support the father will be paying her will be prescribed here.

Check and verify the durations with her state the case is tried in, but she will typically have 30 days from date of order to file a motion for reconsideration to the judge; and 45 calendar days from date of order to file an appeal. She will want to check herself on how she reacts at this point. Her entire case has been built upon allegations of the father raping his children. If she is needing to ask for a reconsideration or make an appeal, she very likely will only make matters worse at this point by questioning the judge's carefully weighed as much in her favor decision. She should by all mean file a motion for reconsideration for things such as but not limited to numerical errors on child support.

If the father has survived her dozens of allegations and received any form of non-supervised visitation, the judge could not completely swing the case in the mother's favor but did as much as possible. Therefore, the mother should lean heavily on her support group, regroup, and bide her time carefully planning a next allegation. Take some time to create new plots to never stop trying to destroy the father. He will not enjoy paying a red cent to someone that uses his children and has put him through what she has. If the judge has granted joint custody in this high conflict case, the judge has likely divided up primary decision maker of certain critical areas.

If the judge has granted the mother Academic decision making, consider relocating somewhere within what that state deems reasonable, usually between 50 and 100 miles. Consider relocating the children to a better school district so that will be her rationale for the move and keep it a little under the maximum distance her state states. Every additional mile the father must drive his children back and forth to school will wear him down.

If the mother receives athletic decision making, become a soccer mom and get them active to where he is responsible for taking them to many events during his time with the children. This takes him away from making additional money for him to defend himself and rebuild. His existence remains fragile. And ultimately, begin working on her next allegation.

When she brings the children to the children exchanges, park in different locations. The mother needs to make changes to precedents and control as many aspects of everything that she can. The mother does things such as not allowing the children to leave her car until hours later. She does everything she can to create a situation where he can place even one finger on her. She points to her feet and orders the father to come stand right there before she will permit the children to exit her car. The mother tries to get the father within arm's reach of her so that she can fall into his arms. The mother knows that if she can have even one witness that he placed a single finger on her she will be able to claim assault. She enjoys all of the numerous options at her fingertips.

CONCLUSION

Moving Forward Post Divorce

The mother is now divorced and has custody of her children. Perhaps the father has survived and not been entirely removed from the picture behind bars or six feet under, but she has committed her life to ruin his. The mother is not finished. The mother will not permit him to survive her agenda. Continue creating chaos everywhere possible. Influence everyone she can. Campaign without end.

The father had to fund her campaign against him throughout the divorce process. He had to pay for his own attorneys as well as the attorneys she went through. She may have grown impatient at times through the long process, but she drained him and his allies of most, if not all, of their resources. The long amount of time likely also provided her a beneficial surpassing of statute of limitations on her allegations to law enforcement if they even took notice of it. The judge will usually ensure law enforcement does not pursue charges against her for filing these allegations. The statute of limitations for that it is as little as one year, depending on her state. The investigations will monopolize most of this time, but a criminal matter would also shut down all activity with the divorce, locking custody in place. No one will want to pursue any criminal charges of her during the divorce, especially the father, because this would provide the judge with an opportunity to put the father in a position where he could not have any access to his children until the criminal case is resolved. The same applies for any pursuit of a civil lawsuit on defamation of character, slander, or libel. His attorneys will advise him to not pursue anything during the divorce and custody case because the judge will use this against him saying he is vengeful and cannot possibly coparent with her. Time is one of her primary weapons throughout the process.

The examples shared within this book should not be taken as guaranteed to globally occur the same in different situations. The mother needs to listen to others' experiences. She learns from as many people as she can. She listens to her gut. Each mother maker her own decisions from all of these and other's examples and takes sole responsibility for her choices. Each mother will have to stand behind her own decisions. These are mere observations made by others that are not attorneys, just normal lay people that have lived through these scenarios.

The mother can accuse the father of neglect. She can accuse him of physically and sexually abusing his own children. She can accuse him of isolating her and controlling her access to money. She can report observing different and bizarre behaviors in her children. She can put her children through multiple visits to the doctors to examine their whole bodies, including the most private of areas for no reason other than to use for her agenda. She can request doctors perform probes to test for STDs, using medical procedures to manipulate the child's private areas for the sake of upholding her accusations. She can kill family pets. She seeks every opportunity to lead the father into an outburst. The divorce court provides every opportunity it can for the mother to take everyone and everything away from the father.

The mother will be able to feed her ego through sharing her stories with the community. She will be able to testify multiple times that all authorities including but not limited to the Child Protective Services, the Child Advocacy Center, Public Prosecutors, Chief Magistrate, Law Enforcement Detectives, Deputies, multiple Doctors, Psychiatrists, Guardian ad litem, teachers, and attorneys are all untrustworthy and inept at performing their sole task of protecting people, especially innocent children. She will likely quickly notice how the judge will not allow anyone to hold her accountable. Perhaps the father will survive her allegations for a

CRAFT HIS FALL AND TAKE IT ALL

while, but he will lose all his money, lose time with his children, be isolated, have a ruined named within his community, and will be left in debt for decades if not life.

Several mothers have had success with using future romantic relationships to assist their case. Throughout the divorce and custody trial the mother maintains a secrecy of her romantic relationships. The mother understood it was important to not provide the father's attorneys any opportunity to claim instability concerning the mother's multiple partners. Several mothers kept their physical needs satisfied with their older women friends before they moved back into men again. However, once the custody order was finalized the mother brings a easily manipulated man she has held in reserve to the custody exchanges. She has shared her accusations with this man motivating him to stand as a physical obstacle between the father and his children. The mother's goal was to have this new man coax the father into an altercation. The court would eagerly amend a custody order if the mother succeeded at gaining a physical altercation from the father. However, if the father does not provide a negative response, and decides to report this man threatening him at the custody exchange, the mother and her attorney were able to report to the judge that the father is a jealous ex-husband that is trying to prevent her from moving on with her life.

The mother never gives up. She faces no accountability. Like many leaders before her, she too can cross the Rubicon and never look back. She is a beacon, empowering others to craft their husbands' fall, so that they too can take it all. The legal system enables such undue processes providing judges the means to rule on emotion rather than fact, to control the narrative when investigations begin to circle back on the mother with an agenda. While the American judicial system provides such options, why should every mother not be made aware and take advantage of it as well? Everyone is always told children are resilient, so why not use them to get the life she deserves?

When the mother finally succeeds, the father will die homeless or live the remainder of his life in prison. She will never have to share custody with him. With the father completely removed her children will eventually give in to her allegations about their daddy, or maybe not, but it will be of no consequence. Between her perfected story and charismatic influence people will always flock to help her. The mother will succeed at crafting his fall and getting it all. And now, to her next host.

You can share your stories, your experiences, your tips and even the occasional unfortunate failures, to the following email address: KarenLeBarron4U@gmail.com

www.ingramcontent.com/pod-product-compliance
Lightning Source LLC
Chambersburg PA
CBHW070642030426
42337CB00020B/4133